HowExp

How To Run a 5k

Your Step By Step Guide To Running a 5K

HowExpert

Copyright HowExpert™
www.HowExpert.com

For more tips related to this topic, visit HowExpert.com/run5k.

Recommended Resources

- HowExpert.com – Quick 'How To' Guides on All Topics from A to Z by Everyday Experts.
- HowExpert.com/free – Free HowExpert Email Newsletter.
- HowExpert.com/books – HowExpert Books
- HowExpert.com/courses – HowExpert Courses
- HowExpert.com/clothing – HowExpert Clothing
- HowExpert.com/membership – HowExpert Membership Site
- HowExpert.com/affiliates – HowExpert Affiliate Program
- HowExpert.com/writers – Write About Your #1 Passion/Knowledge/Expertise & Become a HowExpert Author.
- HowExpert.com/resources – Additional HowExpert Recommended Resources
- YouTube.com/HowExpert – Subscribe to HowExpert YouTube.
- Instagram.com/HowExpert – Follow HowExpert on Instagram.
- Facebook.com/HowExpert – Follow HowExpert on Facebook.

Publisher's Foreword

Dear HowExpert reader,

HowExpert publishes quick 'how to' guides on all topics from A to Z by everyday experts.

At HowExpert, our mission is to discover, empower, and maximize talents of everyday people to ultimately make a positive impact in the world for all topics from A to Z...one everyday expert at a time!

All of our HowExpert guides are written by everyday people just like you and me who have a passion, knowledge, and expertise for a specific topic.

We take great pride in selecting everyday experts who have a passion, great writing skills, and knowledge about a topic that they love to be able to teach you about the topic you are also passionate about and eager to learn about.

We hope you get a lot of value from our HowExpert guides and it can make a positive impact in your life in some kind of way. All of our readers including you altogether help us continue living our mission of making a positive impact in the world for all spheres of influences from A to Z.

If you enjoyed one of our HowExpert guides, then please take a moment to send us your feedback from wherever you got this book.

Thank you and we wish you all the best in all aspects of life.

Sincerely,

BJ Min
Founder & Publisher of HowExpert
HowExpert.com

PS...If you are also interested in becoming a HowExpert author, then please visit our website at HowExpert.com/writers. Thank you & again, all the best!

COPYRIGHT, LEGAL NOTICE AND DISCLAIMER:

COPYRIGHT © BY HOWEXPERT™ (OWNED BY HOT METHODS). ALL RIGHTS RESERVED WORLDWIDE. NO PART OF THIS PUBLICATION MAY BE REPRODUCED IN ANY FORM OR BY ANY MEANS, INCLUDING SCANNING, PHOTOCOPYING, OR OTHERWISE WITHOUT PRIOR WRITTEN PERMISSION OF THE COPYRIGHT HOLDER.

DISCLAIMER AND TERMS OF USE: PLEASE NOTE THAT MUCH OF THIS PUBLICATION IS BASED ON PERSONAL EXPERIENCE AND ANECDOTAL EVIDENCE. ALTHOUGH THE AUTHOR AND PUBLISHER HAVE MADE EVERY REASONABLE ATTEMPT TO ACHIEVE COMPLETE ACCURACY OF THE CONTENT IN THIS GUIDE, THEY ASSUME NO RESPONSIBILITY FOR ERRORS OR OMISSIONS. ALSO, YOU SHOULD USE THIS INFORMATION AS YOU SEE FIT, AND AT YOUR OWN RISK. YOUR PARTICULAR SITUATION MAY NOT BE EXACTLY SUITED TO THE EXAMPLES ILLUSTRATED HERE; IN FACT, IT'S LIKELY THAT THEY WON'T BE THE SAME, AND YOU SHOULD ADJUST YOUR USE OF THE INFORMATION AND RECOMMENDATIONS ACCORDINGLY.

THE AUTHOR AND PUBLISHER DO NOT WARRANT THE PERFORMANCE, EFFECTIVENESS OR APPLICABILITY OF ANY SITES LISTED OR LINKED TO IN THIS BOOK. ALL LINKS ARE FOR INFORMATION PURPOSES ONLY AND ARE NOT WARRANTED FOR CONTENT, ACCURACY OR ANY OTHER IMPLIED OR EXPLICIT PURPOSE.

ANY TRADEMARKS, SERVICE MARKS, PRODUCT NAMES OR NAMED FEATURES ARE ASSUMED TO BE THE PROPERTY OF THEIR RESPECTIVE OWNERS, AND ARE USED ONLY FOR REFERENCE. THERE IS NO IMPLIED ENDORSEMENT IF WE USE ONE OF THESE TERMS.

NO PART OF THIS BOOK MAY BE REPRODUCED, STORED IN A RETRIEVAL SYSTEM, OR TRANSMITTED BY ANY OTHER MEANS: ELECTRONIC, MECHANICAL, PHOTOCOPYING, RECORDING, OR OTHERWISE, WITHOUT THE PRIOR WRITTEN PERMISSION OF THE AUTHOR.

ANY VIOLATION BY STEALING THIS BOOK OR DOWNLOADING OR SHARING IT ILLEGALLY WILL BE PROSECUTED BY LAWYERS TO THE FULLEST EXTENT. THIS PUBLICATION IS PROTECTED UNDER THE US COPYRIGHT ACT OF 1976 AND ALL OTHER APPLICABLE INTERNATIONAL, FEDERAL, STATE AND LOCAL LAWS AND ALL RIGHTS ARE RESERVED, INCLUDING RESALE RIGHTS: YOU ARE NOT ALLOWED TO GIVE OR SELL THIS GUIDE TO ANYONE ELSE.

THIS PUBLICATION IS DESIGNED TO PROVIDE ACCURATE AND AUTHORITATIVE INFORMATION WITH REGARD TO THE SUBJECT MATTER COVERED. IT IS SOLD WITH THE UNDERSTANDING THAT THE AUTHORS AND PUBLISHERS ARE NOT ENGAGED IN RENDERING LEGAL, FINANCIAL, OR OTHER PROFESSIONAL ADVICE. LAWS AND PRACTICES OFTEN VARY FROM STATE TO STATE AND IF LEGAL OR OTHER EXPERT ASSISTANCE IS REQUIRED, THE SERVICES OF A PROFESSIONAL SHOULD BE SOUGHT. THE AUTHORS AND PUBLISHER SPECIFICALLY DISCLAIM ANY LIABILITY THAT IS INCURRED FROM THE USE OR APPLICATION OF THE CONTENTS OF THIS BOOK.

COPYRIGHT BY HOWEXPERT™ (OWNED BY HOT METHODS)
ALL RIGHTS RESERVED WORLDWIDE.

Table of Contents

Recommended Resources 2
Publisher's Foreword 3
Introduction 8
Chapter 1: Before You Get Started 12
Equipment 12
   Clothing 12
   Accessories 15
Shoes 18
   Training Shoes 18
   Racing Shoes/Spikes 22
Chapter 2: Distance Running Basics 26
Breathing 26
Running Form 28
   Body Posture 29
   Arm and Hand Position 30
   Hands! 31
   Legs and Feet 32
The Runner's Mindset 34
The Golden Rules For Running Improvement: 35
   1. Be Moderate With Your Training! 35
   2. Repeat Repeat Repeat!!!!! 36
   3. Stay steady!! 36
   4. Aqua jogging 37

 5. Elliptical Machine 38
 6. Jump Rope 38
 7. Swimming 39
 8. Yoga or Pilates 39
 9. Biking 51
 10. Weightlifting 52
 11. Running on the Beach 53

Chapter 3: Stretch Before and After You Run 55

Stretches to do EVERY time 56

Chapter 4: Drills and Warm-Up 76

Warm-Up Tips And Information 76

Drills 81

Chapter 5: What to Eat, Drink, and Do Before a Workout, Long Run, or Easy Run 100

Chapter 6: Running Schedules (Beginners, Intermediate, and Advanced) 107

Beginner's Schedule: 109

Intermediate Schedule: 113

Advanced Schedule: 119

Chapter 7: Training in Detail 127

Easy Runs: 127

Endurance Runs: 129

Workouts 133

 The Mile Repeat 133

 The Forty Second Sprints 136

    The Easy Run And Strides 138
    The Hill Repeats With Strides 139
   Rest Days and Cross training 141

Chapter 8: Race Day! 142
   What to Bring to the Race 142
    Clothing 142
    Accessories 145
    Food! 147
   Pre-Race Tips 148
   When The Gun Goes Off... 150

Chapter 9: After the Race 153
Recommended Resources 155

Introduction

Typical 5K Race Courses

This guide will show you step-by-step on how to run the 5k race. This guide is helpful for all levels. So, if you are a beginner, intermediate, or advanced runner, you will benefit from this guide because it will help you get started and help you achieve a better running time.

So, let's get started and talk about the basics of the 5k running race.

The 5k is a race that is about 3.1 miles.

It can include a variety of terrains:

- Hills
- Flat surface
- Creeks and other small streams of water
- Clay
- Gravel

- Pavement
- Mud/Dirt
- Grass
- Other

Most races are located in:

- Woods
- Parks

5k races are almost NEVER cancelled due to the weather. Be prepared for the worst-case scenario. Weather conditions include:

- Sun (Can be moderate or extreme)
- Rain
- Snow
- Sleet
- Hail (rarely)

Why run a 5k?

Running in general is very beneficial for one's health, especially for one's heart.

5k is short enough for anyone to have the ability to train for and complete. 5k is long enough to be considered an accomplishment and a long-distance race.

5k races are good starter races for people who want to get a feel for the competitive nature of running; the runners are usually competitive but not diehards. Many collegiate-level and professional runners have also started their careers with a 5k race.

A lot of marathon and half-marathon runners use 5k races for training purposes. They help you gauge your performance in an adrenaline-filled situation. They also serve as good motivators to do better in the future.

What kinds of 5k races are there?

- High school cross country meets (competitions) are 5ks.
- Most community and company sponsored races are run/walk 5k races.

Anyone of any age can run a 5k. Most 5k meets have separate race times for different age groups. Awards usually include overall top male awards, overall top female awards, and age group top awards.

Pre-registration for a 5k race is recommended, although many allow walk-ins to run as well.

Fees?

- The majority of 5k races charge an entrance fee per person. It's typically around $20. However, you can also expect somewhere between $5 and $35. The fee depends on the size of the race, the technology used, the number of staff required, and other factors.
- If you register on the day of the race, there is usually a $5 increase in the fee. Some races are free.

Chapter 1: Before You Get Started

Equipment

- Why is the type of equipment I have important?
    - You can't expect yourself to train and race at your full potential without the right tools to aid you.
    - Look at it this way. Football players wouldn't walk into a game without a helmet, shoulder pads, etc., so why should a runner start a race without proper shoes and clothing?

Clothing

- T-shirts/Tank tops
    - Cotton or cotton and polyester combination
        - Most t-shirts are this type
    - Spandex

- - - Helps to get rid of moisture from sweating
  - o 100% Polyester
    - - My personal favorite, because it's light and keeps you dry and cool.
    - - "Breathable" material
- Long-sleeve shirts
  - o Thin shirts meant for cool summer and autumn mornings or nights
    - - Like Underarmour's "heat gear"
  - o Insulated spandex for cold winter and spring days
    - - Like Underarmour's "cold gear"
- Shorts
  - o Spandex
    - - Tight and aerodynamic
      - - Not always the most comfortable, so you should use these for races only.
  - o Cotton and Polyester
    - - Soft and "breathable"
  - o Running Shorts
    - - Light and very comfortable
    - - My personal favorite

- - - Usually labeled as "running shorts", characterized as having a slight curve on the side. See picture.
- Pants
  - Spandex
    - Skin-tight so doesn't weigh you down.
  - Cotton and spandex
    - A little "bulkier" than spandex but much softer
  - Loose legging-type pants
    - Comfortable but not very aerodynamic
    - Usually not made for racing or running
  - Sweatpants
    - Good for warm-up and stretching
    - DO NOT WEAR FOR RACING!!!
- Sweatshirts/ Hoodies
  - Good for warm-up and stretching
  - Could be worn for racing, but this is not recommended
- Socks

- Cotton or cotton and bamboo (or any other material that allows your feet to "breathe")
- They have socks especially labeled "running", but those are just "breathable" socks with a "running" sign attached and an increased price tag.
  - Just buy the bamboo and cotton combination- it's the kind I recommend the most.

Accessories

- Watch
  - ESSENTIAL!!!
  - Needed for timing workouts, learning to pace, etc.
  - MUST have a timing/stopwatch feature
    - Ideally can do splits (while timing it can split the total time into individual sections so you can tell how fast each distance was).
  - Waterproof

- - - Needed for aqua-jogging and running in the rain, snow, etc.
- Hat
  - Has a top
    - No visors
    - The point is to protect your head from the sun, and without a top it only shields your face.
  - Light color
    - Darker colors like black and navy absorb more light, and they would become hotter.
    - Lighter colors would keep you cooler.
- Sunglasses
  - Protects you from the sun's harmful UV rays
  - Get polarized ones
  - Prevents you from slowing down when the sun glares in your eyes when you run
    - This is an automatic response.
- Headband/Hairband
  - Elastic with no metal parts

- - Some races disqualify for metal parts
  - Holds your hair better
- Pre-Wrap and Athletic Tape
  - Injuries:
    - You must put pre-wrap under athletic tape (or else it will hurt when you take the tape off). And, athletic tape helps if you have an injury or just week joints.
  - Hair:
    - Most races allow you to use pre-wrap as a form of a headband to keep hair out of your face.
      - Wrap it around your upper thigh for sizing, tie the ends, and slip it around your head (it stretches).
- NO JEWELRY
  - Jewelry is never allowed in races.
  - Don't wear loose jewelry when running- even in practice.
    - Could be hazardous if a long necklace or hoop earrings get

caught on something while you are running.
- Some races allow you to put tape over earrings-if they were recently pierced.
- Body jewelry?
  - As long as it isn't seen or has the possibility of hooking onto something

Shoes

Training Shoes

First, you must figure out what type of shoe you need. There are three types of training shoes for running.

Stability-for people who have normal arches on their feet (when they stand most of the pressure is on the middle/outer part of the foot and when they walk the pressure goes towards the ball of the foot). This is called overpronation.

Example of stability shoe – Notice how the middle of the foot to the toe is in pretty much a straight line.

- Motion Controlled- for people who have flat feet (no or very low arches). When standing, the ankles roll inwards and the foot flattens.
- Cushioned- for people who have high arches. When they stand, the pressure is almost exclusively on the outer part of the foot. This is called underpronation.

• Typically, the types of the shoes are labeled, but if not…

- Stability shoes- They are considered to be the "normal" width. A better way to distinguish these are to look at the sole of the shoe. There is usually a line in the middle that runs through the length of the

shoe. If you trace this line with your finger from about the middle of the shoe to the tip it should run in about a straight line (It'll be a little bit of a curve but not too much).
- Cushioned shoes- These shoes look a lot narrower than the stability shoes and the motion-controlled shoes. They are called cushioned shoes because they offer extra cushion to help absorb the shock that occurs when you run. Underpronators receive more shock to their legs because they stay mostly on the outer part of the foot.
- Motion controlled shoes are a lot wider than stability shoes or cushioned shoes. Overpronators' feet roll too much inward- thus too much motion, so these shoes help to lessen the rolling motion.

- Overpronators and Underpronators can wear stability shoes if they get orthotics.
  - Custom-made orthotics work the best.
    - Made to fit your feet exactly and give you just as much support or lack of

> > support to make your foot motion normalized.
> > - Cost about $400 initially and need to be "resoled" every two years (or whenever they wear out) for $60
> > - I recommend them. They are worth it!
> - Can also use the store-made "orthotics"
>   - Basically, insoles with arch support
>   - Good store-made orthotics cost about $30-$40, but must be changed pretty frequently (depends on use)
- Training Shoe Brands I Recommend– very reliable and well-built
  - Brooks
  - Asics
  - Saucony
  - New Balance
  - Nike
- Training Shoe Brands I Would NOT Recommend- seem to invite injuries
  - Puma
  - Underarmour
  - Adidas

For training shoes meant for distance (which 5k is), get a ½ size up from the shoe size you normally buy. You want a ½ size up because of the different terrains you will train on like hills.

The shoe store personnel that are "specially trained" in shoe fitting will not suggest this, as most of them are not 5k runners.

Bottom line for training shoes: I only trust Brooks or Asics for my training shoes. The right training shoes can help to prevent injuries, while the wrong training shoes can get you injured before you even step on the start-line.

Training shoes are more important than racing shoes. You can always race with training shoes but you can never train with racing shoes.

Invest in some good training shoes. It will be worth it in the end.

Racing Shoes/Spikes

When you are buying racing shoes, there are two types:
- Racing flats- lightweight shoes (basically a lighter and less-cushioned training shoe)
    - Good for a course that will be mostly gravel or pavement

- - Some people prefer flats on all courses because they are very light- lighter than spikes.
- Spikes- lightweight shoes with metal spikes in the bottom
  - Especially useful on courses with hills, creeks, mud, and dirt.
  - Can be used if the course only contains a little portion of gravel or pavement.
  - The only downside there is the noise when the metal hits the ground, which dulls the metal too.
  - The metal part of the spikes can be easily replaced- they are part screw part spike.
  - NOT good if the course is mostly pavement or gravel.
  - The more spikes/ spike holes on the bottom the shoe, the better.

Make sure the spikes/ racing flats are mostly mesh material. This gives the shoe the ability to "breathe" and helps to keep it lighter and much more comfortable. This also helps with water drainage after you run through a creek or puddle.

I would recommend choosing spikes over racing flats. They keep you from falling in muddy areas and help you grip hills better so you can get up them faster.

My Recommended Flats and Spikes- have enough cushion to sustain you through the race but not too much as to weigh you down

- Asics
- Brooks
- Nike

Bottom line for racing shoes: When it comes down to it, I would get Asics spikes.

When you tie your running shoes (training or racing), you want to always double knot it, because you don't want to have to retie it. And, make sure you do not tie it too tight or too loose; either of those would put excess strain on your ankles.

The way to tell if it's the correct tightness is to wiggle your toes and try to move your feet up and down. If it's too tight you will have to put a lot of effort into wiggling your feet around, and if it's too loose your feet will easily move. You want to have to put a slight bit of pressure in order to move your feet. This guarantees the right amount of support and flexibility.

Some people like to tuck their shoe strings (after double knotting them) into the sides of their shoe or under the tongue to make sure they don't fall out if they become untied. This is up to you; it won't hurt to do it.

Chapter 2: Distance Running Basics

Before you start your actual training for the 5k, you will need to know some distance running basics.

You may think running is easy and something everybody is born with the ability to do, but not everybody can run correctly.

Before you can be a great runner, you must master the basics. Learning how to run is just as important as actually running.

Breathing

When you run there is a specific way of breathing. You cannot simply breathe in and out. You need to get as much oxygen to your muscles as possible and you need to relax your body.

You must breathe in your nose and out your mouth. Simple right? Well, most people only breathe through their mouths when running, which is why you get panting. When you breathe in your nose and out your mouth, you more efficiently and in a larger quantity get oxygen into your body. Your muscles need to receive oxygen- especially when they are being worked really hard when you run.

When you breathe, you want to draw out the process as long as you can by breathing in as

much as you can/ as long as you can and breathing out as long as you can.

This relaxes your body and your muscles and allows more oxygen to be taken in.

- **A good exercise to practice this with is diaphragmatic breathing:**
    - Stand up straight or sit up straight (with good posture), and close your eyes. Breathe in slowly and count to ten as you are breathing in. After those ten seconds, hold your breath for two to three seconds. Then, slowly breathe out for ten seconds. Do this repeatedly. You should feel relaxed after this, which is how your breathing in a race should make you feel.
- **Another good exercise is The Runner's 100**
    - Lay flat on the ground, and raise your legs up to a six inches position (six inches off the ground). Raise your torso into a crunch position. Your arms should be at your side; now raise them so they are a little above your torso. Now pump your arms up and down at a steady yet quick pace. At the same time practice breathing 5 short and

quick breaths in and 5 breaths out. Repeat this type of breathing twenty times, with your arms in sync with your breathing. When you are finished, you have completed 100 breaths and 100 arm "dips". This exercise works your abdominals (especially needed to run up hills), arms (needed to "pump" when you run), and allows you to learn to even out your breathing while exercising.

Running Form

When you run a 5k, you want to have good running form. This will make your movements a lot smoother, and you will save a lot of effort.

Rule of Thumb: STAY RELAXED. It will make everything a lot easier.

Body Posture

When you run, you should have good posture, meaning you should not be slouched. You don't have to be ram-rod straight, but you must be standing up straight.

The way to determine the exact amount of straight and relaxation is to stand up as straight as you can and push your shoulders as far back as you can. Hold this position for 5 seconds. Let go of your shoulders, but keep your back position. This should feel relaxed yet straight. This is the position your body should be in when you race.

Your head should not lean forwards or back. It should sit straight on top of your shoulders. Try look straight ahead and then bringing your head down a tiny notch. This should be the perfect position for you to hold you head when running.

Staring at the sky or at the ground will slow down your running because it's an automatic response to slow down if you can't see where you are going. If you have to lean towards one of the positions, it's better to look more towards the ground than the sky. Looking towards the ground will at least make sure you won't trip over something.

When running up or down hills, you want to lean forwards a little bit. Running up hills, it will help you get a better grip on the hill and just over all "dig into it" more so you can run up it easier. Running down hills, you want to

lean forward a little more. It will help you "fly" down the hill faster.

Relax. It may feel like you will fall, but most likely you will not. Think of it as a part of the race where you don't have to use effort but can cover a lot of distance. Let gravity take you down the hill. Don't hold back.

When running through a creek or any other small source of water, you want to make sure you keep your torso tall and upright. Do NOT lean here. You want to "cut" through the water as well as possible to save effort while making your way through.

Arm and Hand Position

Your arm should be kept at about a little less than a 90-degree angle when you run. Do not have it at more than a 90-degree angle. That will slow you down.

Pump your arms! By pumping, I mean work them. When you run your arms must be moving back and forth. You may think you can run without your arms, which you can, but you can run so much more efficiently and faster with your arms.

Think of your arms as the wheels of a train. They have to cycle through. It's key to the train/ you running. Imagine a rope in front of you, and your arms have to jet out to grab onto the rope to pull yourself forward.

Whatever you have to do, just make sure you are pumping your arms. The rate and the intensity you pump your arms is directly related to what your legs do, so keep that in mind!

When going uphill, you should pump your arms with even more intensity. Shove them in upward motions as you run up the hill. This will put a little bit of "bounce" in your step as you go up the hill, which helps you run faster.

When going downhill, you need to relax your arms. A lot of people tense up when they see a hill, but don't be afraid. You won't fall. Keep your arms loose but not too loose. Some people let their arms flail when they go downhill, but you need to keep them at your side, relaxed. The swinging should naturally be a bit more exaggerated here.

Hands!

Your hands can be in two different positions:
- Straight out in a rigid position
- Curved naturally- however your hand lies without you thinking about it.

Some people prefer the straight position, because they believe it's more aerodynamic and puts them in more of a focused mood.

I personally use the curved hand position, because it takes less effort and energy. Try running a mile with each of the positions and decide which is best for you.

There is no right or wrong here. I have seen professionals take both sides. It just matters what you feel more comfortable doing.

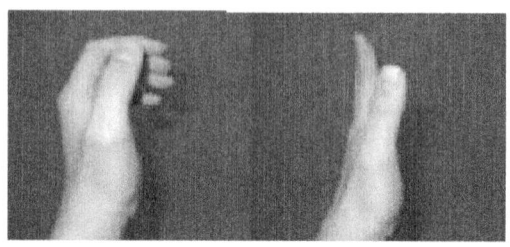

Legs and Feet

When you run, you want a fast turnover rate. This means you want your legs to cycle through fast. You don't necessarily need to raise your legs really fast. Actually, I would advise against bringing your leg up faster than necessary- you would just be using more energy. It's more important to bring your leg and foot down as fast as possible.

When running on a flat surface, you should bring your leg straight up and then stick your leg straight out from there. This will give you a long stride. Basically, this will allow you to cover more distance in each step and with less effort.

A good drill to practice this with is if you exaggerate these movements. On flat ground, you would bring your knee up so it's a 90-degree angle, and then you would extend your leg straight out. Then, you would very quickly drop your leg (more like shove your foot into the ground with a lot of force to it makes a shuffling sound when it hits the floor). Alternate this between your feet for about 15 repetitions.

When running up a hill, you should bring your knees up higher, to about a 90-degree angle. This is the equivalent of a longer stride on a flat surface, because this allows you to cover more ground. You should also run on either your toes or the balls of your feet. I prefer running on my toes, but for long hills it is a lot more difficult to do so. I recommend running on your toes for as long as possible and switch to the balls of your feet as a second option.

While running on your toes, your body should automatically lean a bit towards the hill. If you do not notice this, then you should purposely lean a little bit towards the hill.

Shorten your stride (the distance between your steps) as you approach a hill and start to a faster turnover for your feet. This will help you run up the hill a lot faster. (It may feel like a lot more effort, but it will get you over the hill sooner.)

When running down a hill, you want to make sure you're on your toes. It will not put too much strain on your foot here, because gravity is pulling you down. Your feet should automatically land on your toes to "catch" yourself while you are flying down the hill. Make sure you DO NOT let your heels strike the ground when you are going downhill. Every time your heel strikes the ground in this situation, it is like putting the brakes on. It will only slow you down. So, stay on your toes!

When running in creeks or any small source of water, you want to make sure you bring your knees higher than normal. This is what is called "doing high knees". Just bring them up so they are perpendicular to your body and form a 90-degree angle.

This easily becomes tiring –especially with the weight of the water added, so you should try doing high knee drills. On a flat surface, bring your knees up to 90 degrees and jog like that for about 15 repetitions. More or less doesn't matter. As time goes on, you should increase this amount- you never know how large or long a creek or stream may be!

General Rule for Running: Keep good posture, look straight ahead, keep your arms swinging naturally at your sides, and run on the ball of your foot. Some people prefer to strike first- on flat ground- with their heels to absorb the impact. I recommend running on the balls of your feet- at least as much as possible, because your heels will always serve as brakes (although not as much on flat ground as they do on hills).

The Runner's Mindset

As a runner you have to have "the runner's mindset". This means that you have to be realistic about your results and you have to think positively. This may sound cliché, but in reality, it could affect your running.

If you think you won't do well, you won't. You already blew it before you started. Think in terms of what you have accomplished rather than what you haven't. If you don't reward yourself for your efforts, you will never be able to make it through to success- trust me. You can't get through plateaus (times when you train and train but do not get any better), injuries, or stressful competitions without the right mentality.

It's easier to achieve the mindset if you understand how you will get better.

The Golden Rules For Running Improvement:

1. *Be Moderate With Your Training!*

- Your training schedule should always include both hard workouts and easy runs.

    - If you only do hard workouts, your body will not have the chance to recover. Then, you will end up with an injury, not improve, or both!

- If you only do easy runs, then you will never have the chance to truly improve your speed. Your increase in mileage will help you endure the race, but it will not help you do well in the race.

2. Repeat Repeat Repeat!!!!!

- You must repeat the workouts and easy runs you do!!!!
  - You can't expect yourself to improve at one aspect if you only try the training session once! (Not to mention improving at something boosts your mentality, which is important for runners).
  - Easy runs with the same distance each time will become easier and easier as you get into better and better shape. They will become enjoyable- if they aren't already, and no one wants to run if it's all "work".

3. Stay steady!!

- Practice makes perfect OVER TIME.

- Increase mileage and speed a little bit at a time. "Too much too fast" will only cause injuries.

4. *Aqua jogging*

- Basically, this is running in the water. Find a pool or lake or any body of water that is deep enough that you cannot touch the bottom. You can purchase an official "aqua jogger" or buy some sort of flotation device that will go around your waist. When you go in the water, you can do the same motions as when you run. This will be much harder because the water provides resistance- you build muscle and don't have to spend as much time in the water to get the results. To simulate running up hills while aqua jogging, you simply straighten your legs and kick upwards with straightened legs. No impact, but can strain weak joints such as ankles.

5. Elliptical Machine

- This is good for tired or injured joints. There is virtually no impact and does not strain any joints or muscles.
- You can read a book or magazine or watch TV at the same time!
- Ten minutes on this usually about simulates 1 mile on the ground

6. Jump Rope

- If done for about 3-5 minutes intervals it helps with endurance. It also trains your arms; the motion simulates the swinging motion done when running.
    - Do about 4-6 repetitions. Increase the amount as needed.
- You don't actually need a jump rope for this exercise. Simply doing the motions usually is good enough for beginners to early intermediate (easily replaces a standard jump rope without weights). More advanced people should get a jump rope with weights for a better workout.

7. Swimming

Swimming works all of your muscles, and when you run, most of your muscles are being used.

- Swimming has no impact, so it provides a good break for your joints after a lot of running.
- Any type of stroke is acceptable.
- Treading water by itself is also very beneficial.
- For a more advanced variation on treading water, try holding your arms straight up and out of the water while treading. Do this for as long as possible.

8. Yoga or Pilates

- I recommend making room once a week for a Yoga and Pilates combination.
- This is good to stretch out your muscles and to also strengthen your muscles.
- The most important exercise in Pilates for runners is The Plank. It helps to strengthen your core, which is essential for running up hills and having long strides.

- There are several levels and variations for the plank.
    - For the basic one, you start out lying flat on your stomach on the floor. Slowly get into a pushup position. Then, you lower yourself onto your forearms. Your palms can be flat on the floor or your hands can be in fists that come together to form the point of a triangle. Make sure your body is in a straight line, and pull your stomach and abs in to stabilize the entire position. Hold this for 30 seconds (for beginners) and up to 60 seconds for more advanced people. After you can hold it 60 seconds, you should go to a more advanced level.

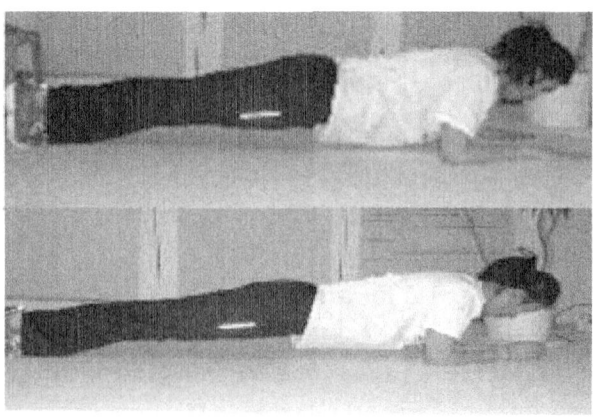

**Top: One leg in front of the other
Bottom: One leg on top of the other**

- For the next level up, you would start lying on your side. Leaning on one forearm, you would raise yourself into something like a sideways pushup position. Place on foot in front of the other for balance. The arm not on the floor should be raised straight up into the air. Hold for 30-60 seconds. After you can do 60 seconds, advance by stacking both feet. This makes the balance more difficult and thus challenges your core a bit more.
- An even more challenging plank position would entail starting in the basic plank position with your

palms flat on the floor and then shifting your weight from your forearms to your palms as you raise yourself into a pushup position. This should be done while maintaining your stability- excess wobbling should not occur. Do this about 15 times- if you cannot then slowly work your way up to that number.

- All of these plank exercises should be done with a lot of control. Too much wobbling or instability indicates the exercise is too difficult for your core at that time, and you should try an easier level.
- Another important Pilates exercise is the "Superman".
    - You lie flat on the floor on your stomach, and you extend your arms and legs straight out. Then, you raise your arms (with your torso) and your legs about 6 inches off the ground. Hold this for 30 seconds- 1 minute (depending on your level).

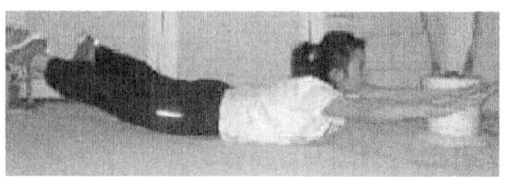

- If you cannot yet do the Superman for 30 seconds, you should break the exercise up and try the Trunk Lift and Six Inches.
    - The trunk lift is when you lie flat on the floor on your stomach with your arms at your sides and you lift your torso and your head up to about 6 inches (can be more but 6 inches here to correspond with the "Superman").

    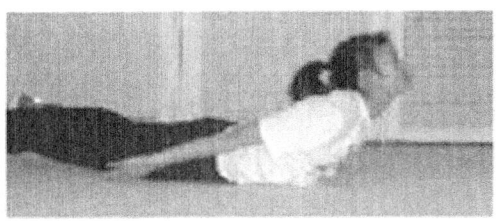

    - Six Inches is when you lie flat on the floor on your back and you lift your legs straight up into the air until they are about 6 inches off the ground. Hold this there for one minute (can be more but one minute here to correspond with the "Superman").

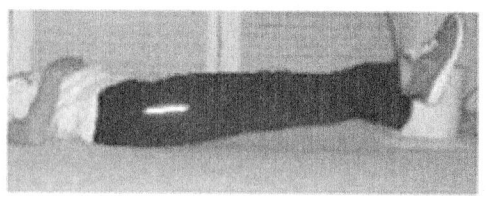

- Another Pilates exercise for the abdominal muscles and core muscles, which are much needed for running hills, is the "Windshield Wiper".
    - You want to start lying on the ground on your back. Spread both arms out so they extend straight out at your sides. Lift your legs (keep them together and straight) straight up so it's perpendicular to your body.
    - In a controlled motion, use your abdominals to bring your legs to the side (almost to the floor) and then back to the original straight up position. Bring it to the other side the same way and "pull" them back to the center position.
    - Repeat this 15-30 times based on experience and how many you are able to do. If you need a break in the middle, bring your legs back to the center position (straight up) and rest there.

- (Picture below)

- Another Pilates exercise aimed at your abdominals and core muscles is what is called "The Runner's Crunch".
    - Lay on the floor on your back with you knee bent and feet resting flat on the floor. Pick up on leg and bend and fold it sideways so your foot is resting on the other leg. Put your hands behind your ears (this way you won't be able to use your hands at all to help you perform the crunch- they only help to support your head). Crunch sideways aiming your shoulder (not just your arms) opposite of the bent knee towards the knee. Do 15 of the crunches, and then switch legs and shoulders.
    - Remember you are always crunching towards the opposite knee.

- A variation on this: Lie on the floor on your back and bend both knees. Lift them off the ground until they form a 90-degree angle. This position is called "table top". The hand and arm position for this is a little different. Bend your elbows and make a relaxed "fist" on your hands. Place the knuckle portion of your hands against your forehead and crunch until your elbow hit your thighs (if done straight up).
  - You can go up either straight or twist for this as well.

- For Yoga, there are a couple of key stretches/exercises that I make sure to always include helping with relaxation.
    - The Child Position
        - My personal favorite.
        - It is a very simple Yoga pose, but it is very effective (if done correctly) in relaxing you.
        - Start in a kneeling position and lower yourself until you are sitting on your feet. Then, lower your torso and upper body until you are in a bowing position. You can outstretch your arms or leave them by your sides. Close your eyes and take several deep breaths. In your nose and out your mouth just like when you are running, and don't forget to elongate them as much as possible.

- The Tree Position
    - This is also a relatively simple Yoga position, but it is a good exercise for balance. It also involves some of your core muscles if you are to do it right, and both are essential in running.
    - Start by standing straight with your hands by your sides- and with good posture! Raise your one leg, and tuck the foot so it rests on the side of the other leg's thigh. Steady yourself (with a wall or chair if needed). Then slowly bring your hands up from the sides until they meet above your head, palms together. This should resemble a tree. Close your eyes and take several slow, deep breaths (in your nose and out your mouth).

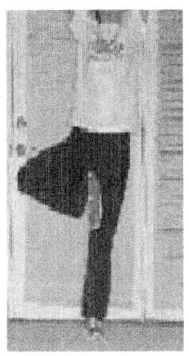

- Downwards Dog
  - This position is easy to do, relaxing, and great for stretching out your legs.
  - Start in a push up position. Slowly walk your feet and legs forwards until you feel a slight stretch in your legs. You should not walk your feet all the way up to the point where they are right next to your hands. You want to maintain the pushup position structure, but form more of a triangle shape with your body. Now, lean your entire body backwards so the focus is on your legs. You should feel a more intense stretch now. Close your eyes and take

a couple of deep breaths. Relax for a couple of seconds by going back to that triangle shape without leaning backwards.
- Repeat this about 6 times.

- Triangle Position
  - This is a very simple pose (almost as simple as The Child Position).
  - Start standing. You want your feet to be a little wider than shoulder width apart. You want a nice, firm stance. Reach your hands straight up and then lean over to one side so one of your arms is resting on one of your legs and the other is still outstretched in the air. Close your eyes and breathe deeply. Return to the position where both arms are in

the air and do the same with the other arm and leg.
- Repeat this about 6 times.

  o For Yoga, I would especially recommend using a yoga mat as the positions can sometimes be hard to maintain if you are slipping.

9. *Biking*

- Biking is another no impact alternative to running. I often replace one easy run a week with a biking session. It can be indoors or outdoors, on a stationary bike or not.

- I generally treat ten minutes of biking as the equivalence of one mile of running.
- If possible, make sure you increase the resistance of the bike so as the bike ride is not TOO easy.

10. *Weightlifting*

- Any type of weightlifting is highly beneficial for runners.
- On your easy run days, I recommend adding some weightlifting into the routine (even if it is just a little bit).
    - Not at the same time- this will strain your muscles and possibly lead to an injury. For example, run in the morning and lift in the evening.
- I recommend mostly focusing on arms and legs when weightlifting. Other muscles can be worked as well, but these should be where the emphasis is on.
- When weightlifting, make sure you are doing less weight with more repetition. This will get you toned, and that is what you need for running.

Heavier weights with less repetitions help you "bulk" up (with muscle over fat); this will just give you more weight to carry while you run, which will slow you down.

11. *Running on the Beach*

- If you are by the beach and prefer to run in the sand, then here are some tips to remember.
- Run without shoes. If you run with shoes, sand will get into it and weigh you down. In addition, it's pretty annoying to have sand in your shoes.
- Don't start out by running a lot in the sand if you haven't done it much before. Sand sinks, so it's an unstable terrain. This puts pressure on all (or most) of your joints in your legs; most importantly on your ankles and knees.
  - Instead, slowly ease yourself onto running in the sand. Maybe one mile (or the time equivalence if you know how fast you typically can run a mile) one day and a mile and increase it to a mile and a half two days later.
- Watch out for sharp objects like seashells or rocks!

- Running barefoot makes it a lot easier to cut your feet or injury yourself.
- Just be careful!

Chapter 3: Stretch Before and After You Run

You always need to make sure you stretch!!

Stretches are just as important as workouts and actual running. Without stretching you put yourself in a compromising position and at high risk for injury. If you are injured you will either not run your best 5k or not be able to run the race at all.

I always stretch immediately before I begin to run and immediately afterwards. Some people prefer to stretch after a warm-up and after a cool-down. Either way it seems to work.

Some new research claims that you don't need to stretch before you run, only afterwards. However, I highly recommend you always stretch in the beginning. It loosens and warms up your muscles to get them ready to run, and that aspect helps to prevent injuries. It wouldn't hurt anyways.

- Hold all stretches for about 15 seconds. Holding it for a bit longer than 15 seconds is okay, but do NOT hold it for any less than 10 seconds. You do not want to be "bouncing", because that will just harm your muscle and perhaps cause an injury. Repeat this 3-6 times on each muscle with about 7 seconds to rest or relax your muscles in between.

Stretching should NEVER hurt. If it hurts, then you MUST STOP. If your muscle is a little tight, then you would just feel very minor discomfort as your muscles loosen up during the stretch. This is what stretching is for.

Stretches to do EVERY time

- Don't forget to touch your toes!
- The most basic version: Sit on the ground with your legs straight out and reach to your toes with both of your hands. Hold this position for 15 seconds. Repeat.
    - A little bit more of a stretch: While sitting on the ground, bend one knee and keep the other knee straight. Let the bent knee drop so it is resting on the ground, still bent. Then, use both hands and reach towards the one outstretched foot. Hold the position for 15 seconds. Repeat 3 times. Do the same for the other foot.

- If you want to avoid sitting on the ground: Stand with your feet a great bit wider apart than shoulder width. Then reach down with both arms to touch the toes on one side. Hold for 15 seconds. Repeat 3 times. Switch to the other leg and do the same.
- Start standing with one leg crossed over the other. Put both arms together and try to touch your toes. Hold for 15 seconds and repeat 3 times. Cross your legs the other way and repeat.
- Make like a Flamingo!
  - Start standing. If you have balance issues it may be beneficial to be near a wall or chair. Bend one leg at the knee and use the same arm (same

side of the body) or the opposite arm to catch it and pull it back more for even more of a stretch. Some people claim that using different arms stretches uses different muscles, but in the end, it doesn't really make that much of a difference, so I wouldn't worry about it. Hold for 15 seconds, relax for 5 seconds, and repeat 4 times. Change legs (or arms if you feel the need to) and repeat.

- From a sideways view, your legs make the "four" that flamingos make. Thus, why this stretch is often called the flamingo.

- What about the calves?!?
    - There are a couple of different exercises I commonly use. I recommend switching it up and choosing two each day- in any combination. It is ESSENTIAL to stretch your calves, because a lot of common runner's injuries are related to some sort of calf muscle (ex. The Achilles tendon, shin splints, tibia/fibia fractures or stress fractures, etc.).
    - Start standing about an arm's length from a wall. Face the wall, and place both palms against the wall. Flex one

of your feet and place the toes against the bottom of the wall, with your heels still on the ground. Lean into the wall, and you should feel a stretch in your calves. Hold for 15 seconds, relax 6 seconds, and repeat 5 times. Switch legs and do the same again.

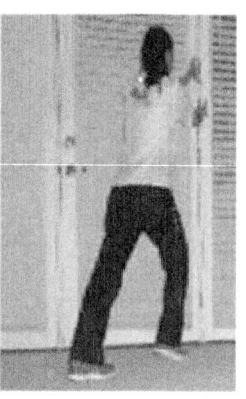

- In the same position as the one above (palms on the wall and toes leaning on the wall), simply add a slight squat into the stretch. Bend your knees ever slightly, and you should feel a stretch in a deeper part of your calf. This stretches the muscles in the more interior part of your leg, which are often neglected.

- About an arm's length from the wall- same as the other exercise, keep both feet flat on the floor. Press your palms on the wall, for more of a stretch, and place one foot closer to the wall and one further away. Straighten the back leg and bend the front leg (closest to the wall). Lean onto your hands on the wall. Hold for 15 seconds, rest 3, and repeat 4-5 times.
- Find an elevated surface like a stair step where you can hang your heels off the end of. This stretches the lower part of your calf and your Achilles tendon, which is often injured and is pretty painful. Step onto the elevated surface with your toes. Your heels should be in the air. Lower heels until you feel a stretch. You may want to hold onto a wall or something for balance, although it is

not necessary. Hold for 12 seconds (the tendon is often a lot tighter than most others and you wouldn't want to put too much strain on it) and relax for 8 seconds. Repeat this about 5 times.

- Prevent Shin Splints! Or aid the healing process! Try a simple stretching exercise to stretch the muscles are your shins. Raise one leg off the ground and point your leg straight out. Make sure you point your toes as well. Then, turn your foot inwards- towards the other foot. Hold this for 15 seconds. Rest for 3 seconds and repeat 3-4 times. Do this once or twice a day (twice if you already have shin splints or a shin/tibia area injured).

- Fly like a butterfly!
    - Sit on the ground in a crisscrossed or "Indian style" to start. Place the bottoms of your feet together. Bring your feet in closer to your body until your thighs are bent and in the air. From here you want to push down your thighs (without your hands) as far as you can go. Hold for 20 seconds. Rest for 4 seconds and repeat 4 times.
    - You can do the traditional way or a different variation with just about the same results. It is just a little more fun. In the same position, simulate a butterfly by releasing and

pushing your thighs down continuously. Thus, you make your legs "flap" like a butterfly, which is why this stretch is called the butterfly.

- Remember to Twist!!

    o Your back should also be stretched before and after you run; although most people forget this aspect, and that's why you get the back pain. Combined with incorrect running form, this is a recipe for disaster- or an injury.

    o Start by sitting on the ground with your legs extended straight out. Bend one knee and cross it over the other leg that is still extended straight out. Now twist at your waist in the direction of the leg that is bent. Twist your entire torso/upper body. Your arms should go along with the twist. You should be facing sideways compared to your legs, with your inner most arm resting on the bent knee. Use the ground to push yourself into a deeper stretch. Hold for 20 seconds. Rest/relax by loosening the "twist" part for about 5 seconds. Repeat 3-4 times.

- Weak ankles? If not, I'd still recommend doing the following exercises as a precaution.
    - Weak ankles are very susceptible to injuries. This is why you hear a lot about sprained and twisted ankles from running- and not just because of a fall.

- Do each of these exercises once a day. If that's not possible then randomly pick 2 of them each day to perform.

- While standing, shift all of your weight onto your toes. Keep this position for 12 seconds while maintaining your balance. A chair or wall may be used as well. Rest for 5 seconds and repeat 5 times.

- While standing, shift all of your weight onto one foot and lift the other foot off of the ground. Hold this position for 20 seconds. Rest for 5 seconds and repeat 4 times. Switch feet and do the same for the other side.

- While sitting (or standing if you have good balance or a wall), extend one foot straight out. Point your toes and "trace the alphabet" with your foot. Bend and rotate your foot at your ankle to draw imaginary lines to form the alphabet. You can take a break every so often if your ankle becomes tired; I'd recommend only after 10 letters or so to take a break.
    - Does this tracing movement slowly; if it's done too fast it could put strain on your ankles.

- Do the alphabet once or twice on both feet.

- Tracing the alphabet as opposed to just circles helps to flex the ankle and foot in all directions, helping in the strengthening process.

- Just like stretching your neck by rotating in a full circle, doing the same with your ankle may also cause some strain. I would not recommend doing "ankle circles".

o Start by sitting either on the ground or on a chair. Lift one foot and rest your ankle on top of the other leg's thigh. (You want to make sure your other leg is there to support it during this exercise.) With your hand closest to the foot being stretched, grab the top part of the ankle- the part not resting on the other leg. Use the other hand to stabilize your elevated leg by holding the shin or tibia region down. Using the hand on the ankle, gently and slowly guide your ankle through a circular rotation and in all different directions. Do this for about 20 seconds. Rest/relax for 7 seconds. Repeat 3-5 times. Switch ankles and do the same.

- A circular rotation for the ankle is allowed here, because your ankle is resting on your other leg, which provides support for your ankle. Thus, your ankle is relieved of a lot of strain that you would've received otherwise by rotating it.

- This exercise/stretch involves the use of a stretching, exercise, or resistance band. Place one end of the band under a stable chair leg or table leg and the other end around the shoelace part of your foot. Move backwards from the table, while still keeping the band around your foot, until the band is taut or tightly pulled. Then, slowly bend your ankle or "pull" your toes towards you, so you bend your ankle upwards. Hold the position for 12 seconds when you get to the farthest back you can pull your toes back with the resistance band. Rest for 6 seconds and repeat 2 more times. Switch feet and repeat.

- o If you feel a strain in your ankle at all, don't "pull" your foot back as much.
- o How far back your foot can bend or stretch depends on both the strength of your ankle and the strength of the resistance band.
- Try marching!

- The "Roll-step" most marching bands use also strengthens your ankle.

- This is just a little variation on walking. Instead of just putting your feet down one in front of the other as done in walking, you should "roll" your feet. Strive the heel down first and shift the weight to the heel. All weight should be on the foot that is rolling at the time. To make sure this is done right, pick the other foot up after rolling a foot. You should not lose balance if it was done correctly. When roll-stepping, imagine you are walking on a giant tube of toothpaste and you must squeeze the paste out with your feet.

- The shift of weight should be smooth. If you hold a glass full of water in your hands, the water should not spill.

- Arms!

- You need your arms to pump when you're running, so you want to make sure they get their proper stretches in.

- Do ALL or most of these stretches.

- Start by swinging both arms. Swing one- while still extended straight out- across your body to the other side and bend the other arm over it to hold it in that position. Hold for 15 seconds. Rest/relax 3 seconds and repeat 3-4 times. Swing arms again and switch arms. Do the same for the other side.

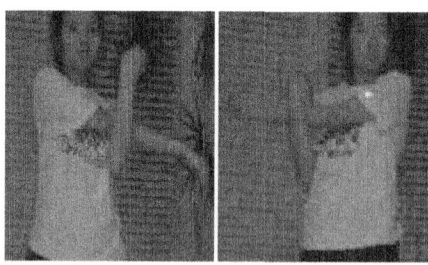

- Extend one arm straight up above your head. Bend it at the elbow, to your forearm and hand is resting on your back. Now take the other hand and grab the bent arm's elbow to pull it in for a stretch. Hold for 12

seconds. Rest for 3 seconds. Repeat 3-4 times. Switch arms.

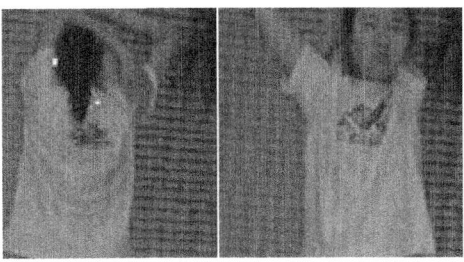

- Extend both of your arms straight out and swing them side to side making sure to cross over each other when they meet directly in front of your torso. For each swing, alternate which arm is on top when they cross each over other.

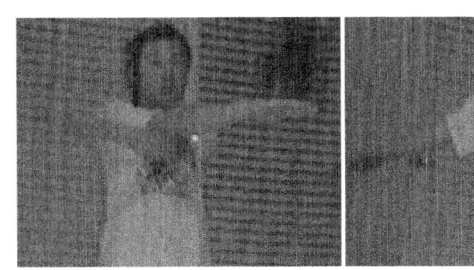

- Extend your arms straight out and put them behind you. Now try to push them as close together (using your shoulder blades) as possible behind your back. When you reach that point hold it for 12 seconds. Rest for 5 seconds and repeat 3 times.

- Arm Circles!

    o   Extend both of your arms straight out and twist them 180 degrees about your shoulders. You should be "drawing" circles in the air. This is for your shoulders mostly.

- Knees!
    o   Make sure you stretch your knees! They receive a lot of impact when you run.
    o   Start sitting on the ground with both legs extended straight out. Leave one straight and bend the other one. Turn the bent leg sideways and grab

it with one of your arm(s). Pull it towards your torso with a bent arm, using your forearm.
- You should feel a stretch here. Hold for 15 seconds. Relax for 4 seconds and repeat 3 times. Switch legs.

- Start sitting on a chair. Leave on leg bent and touching the floor, but bend one leg and rest it on the leg still on the floor. Now lean forward so your torso is hovering over the leg complex we just created. You should now feel a stretch in that knee. Hold for 14-15 seconds. Rest for 5 seconds, and repeat 2-3 times. Switch legs.

Chapter 4: Drills and Warm-Up

Make sure you ALWAYS warm-up before running- any type whether it's an easy run or a race.

Drills are pretty important, but if you are time-strapped they can be skipped.

Technically doing drills are part of warming up, but I consider a warm up when you slowly jog before a run.

Typically, I do drills after a warm-up run. It can be reversed, but I don't recommend it that way.

Warm-Up Tips And Information

Typically, my warm-ups are always one mile to one mile and a half. I don't think you need much more than that, but this could change from person to person.

Do NOT do less than a mile warm-up. Your muscles need sufficient distance to loosen up and "warm" up.

A warm-up is not a race or a workout. There's no need to "beat" anyone or any time. The entire point is to go slow. Don't try to speed up the warm up.

- For beginners I would say about a 15-20-minute mile for the warm-up.

- For intermediate runners, I would recommend about a 10-15-minute mile.
- For advanced or upper intermediate runners, I would say about a 7-10-minute mile.
  - Remember it doesn't matter if you just upgraded to running from walking or if you're destined for the Olympics. Warm-ups are supposed to be slow. Just because you run an 18-minute mile warm up time doesn't mean you're a slow runner.

Don't forget about your running form when running a warm-up. This slow running is a good time to practice running form!

The more you practice the better you get, and after a while it will become a habit and you will do it all the time.

- For a time-less warm-up pace, you should aim for a pace at which you can carry an on-going conversation with someone without really becoming out of breath.
- For a warm-up that's also beneficial, I would recommend doing more than simply getting from point A to point B to finish your warm-up.

- Exaggerate your running motions. Use a lot of arm movements and elongate your strides. This helps your body to get into the habit, which would be less exaggerated when actually done.
- Not necessary if you just want an easy warm-up that's true to its initial purpose.

Try to do your warm-up on a flat and even surface. Hilly terrains and uneven surfaces put strain on your legs, and they cause you to use unnecessary energy.

Warm-ups are supposed to be easy! Don't work yourself too hard. That's what workouts are for! It's better to have a fast work-out than a fast warm-up.

If it's cold outside, you should wear long sleeves and long pants during your warm-up. This is the time for your muscles to loosen and literally warm up.

Many people prefer to wear less clothing during workouts (even when it's cold), because you get really hot and sweaty when you are training and doing workouts.

You CAN stretch in the middle of a warm-up! Stretching is not only reserved for before or after a warm-up. This is the time to get your muscles ready for intense training, so if any of them feel tight then you should stretch or else you would risk an injury.

Sometimes you can continue running your warm-up and the muscle will loosen itself up.

I would recommend stopping to stretch anyways if you're in this situation. Don't take the risk.

Warm-ups are a great time to get familiar with the work-out or easy run you are about to do and key points to remember.

- During a warm-up, I always think about the type of work-out or easy run I am about to do. It's always better to start out knowing exactly what you have to do. You won't be wasting any time. Ask yourself questions like:
    o What's the distance?
    o What should my time be for each particular distance? Be familiar with around the time frame you should have for each. This way you can monitor your progress during the work-out without having to stop to check it.
    o Does this workout require pacing, sprinting, or any other type of special running technique? If so, then how can I get the most out of it?

*Pacing is the type of running you typically run for the most part in the 5k race. This is when you are running at the fastest pace that you can at least keep for the entire 5k or 3.1 miles.

*Sprinting is when you run as fast as you can. This is for short distances. The last part of the 5k should consist of sprinting. (Some people like to sprint for the beginning as well to get "in front", but I think it drains unnecessary energy- especially if you go out too fast.)

- Do I get any breaks? If so, then how long are they each? What type of breaks are they? Slow jogging or complete stop?

- What good is this work-out for? You have to remember what it will specifically help you with in the 5k race. This helps with motivation, and it's always nice to know you aren't running a useless work-out.

- If you are just getting ready to run a long run or an easy run, then you don't have to do this.

Drills

Now that you've finished your warm-up, it's time to do drills to get your body "revved up" for the workout or easy run.

Drills help to teach and practice good running techniques. Often, they involve over exaggerated movements, because later when you are running you usually subconsciously do them but with less exaggeration.

You are allowed to take a break in the middle of a drill. Drills can be tiring, and you don't need to spend all of your energy on the drills. Drills are mostly used for technique; they are not workouts!

Before I run, I make sure to do all of the following drills. I recommend performing all of them or at least most of them. The order does not matter.

- High Knees

    o This is the type of running you have to do when running through water. It is also beneficial to practice this, because the higher you bring your knees up when running, the longer your stride. This is because after you bring your knee up your leg kicks straight out, and a higher kick up will cause a longer stride.

- In place of actually running, you would just bring your knees straight up so it forms a right angle with your body. Make sure each step you take here all consists of that. This will considerably slow down your running- distance wise. In actuality, you should be moving your legs up and down just as fast as if you were actually running- just the energy and motion is more going vertical than horizontal.

- Make sure to the do arm movements along with it!

- For this exercise, you should be "running" on either your toes or the ball of your feet. You don't have to particularly try to do this, but generally this is how it's performed because you want to get your knees up and down as much and as quick as possible. In a race, you want your energy and time to be mostly spent going forward instead of up.

- Do this for about 100m or 328 feet. If you don't know this distance or cannot judge it (Think of a track- regularly they are 400m. One straightaway of the track is 100m), then just do the drill for about 2-3 minutes. That should be about sufficient, and a little more or less does not make that much of a difference.

- Butt Kicks

    - When you run you want a fuller/larger leg cycle. At the other end of the spectrum from the high knees are butt kicks.

- This stretches your hamstrings and helps with running technique.

- Instead of bringing you knees to a 90-degree angle like you did for high knees, bring your legs up behind you so they "kick" your butt. It's the same running action, but you're using the momentum to kick your butt.

- The goal here is not to get to the end of the 100m or 328 feet, but it is to get as much of the "butt kicks" in each distance as possible. In other words, you want to be kicking really fast; it doesn't matter how fast you finish the distance. In fact, if you are doing this right, then you should take a while to get to the other side. Again, this should be done for 2-3 minutes if you cannot measure or estimate the distance.

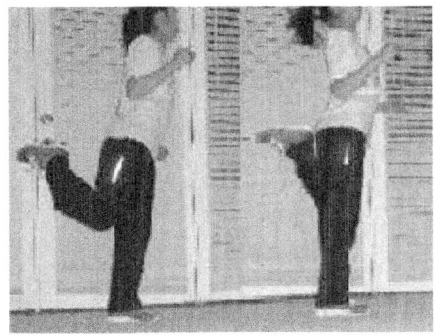

- A's and B's
    - They are part of a two-part series (Part A and Part B) that are useful together to help with the efficient use of energy expenditure in your legs. In other words, they teach you how to move your legs when running so you get the most out of the energy you use.
    - A's
        - When you do this exercise think of a mix between skipping, shuffling, and high knees. For this exercise you will bring one leg up to the 90-degree angle (like in high knees), and this time instead of bringing that down and doing the same with the other leg,

you will leave the same leg up. While the leg is still up, you will do a little one-legged hop. This hop is actually more or a shuffle, as you should be moving forward a lot more than you are moving up- you want to barely get off the ground.
- Think "shuffle".
- Switch legs after each shuffle. If you cannot do this quickly at first, you can "walk" it. As in, you can do it in slow motion the first few times to get a hang of it.
- Do this for about 75 m or 246 feet or time-wise about 2 minutes.

- B's

- This part adds in the bringing your foot down as fast as possible aspect.

- This is a little more difficult than the A's.

- Bring one leg up to the 90-degree angle we have been using. Then extend that leg- from there- straight out. Drop your leg as fast as possible- this usually entails not only letting it fall but forcing it down a little bit as well. It should be a slight scraping sound as it hits the ground. The motion should make your leg automatically go behind you after scraping the ground as well.
Then, switch feet each time. This should be an exaggerated running motion.

- Do this for about 100 m or 328 ft or 2-3 minutes.

- I recommend starters walk this drill first. This is what I did when I first learned the drill. It's better to learn the drill right in the beginning and having to do it slower than wasting your time by doing it fast and wrong.

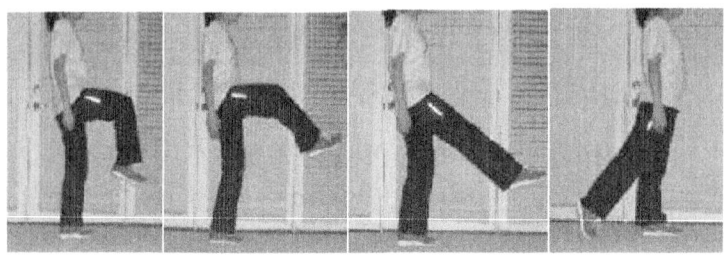

- Hurdler's Drill
    - Don't let the name fool you. As a 5k runner, you will still be doing this drill. It helps with picking your feet up higher when you run, and it's good for stretching.
    - Start by standing. Then, pick one of your legs up and bring it up by circling your leg backwards (counterclockwise) until it is by your side. Your leg's angle from your body should be approach 90

degrees; it's better more than less. (Obviously while you're bringing it up it will be much less than that so don't stress about it.) Alternate legs with this. This should allow the forward motion to occur, although it will be very slow.
- Do this for about 75 m or 246 ft or about 2 ½ min- 3 min (It takes a bit longer, because the forward/backward motion is a lot slower).
- When you finish circling your leg backwards, switch it around so you swing your leg frontwards (clockwise). You should be moving backwards when doing this part. Do this for the same distance.

- Ankle-ing
  - When doing this drill, think about having a "bounce" in your step.
  - In this drill you must stay on the balls of your feet. You want to make a type of circling motion with your foot when you go to take a step each time. Alternate

this from foot to foot as if you were walking.

- Do this for 100 m or 328 ft or about 2 minutes (It covers distance at a pretty good pace.)
- It's a lot like "prancing".
- You will go more sideways than forewords doing this drill.
- Take your time; this should be one of the more fun drills.

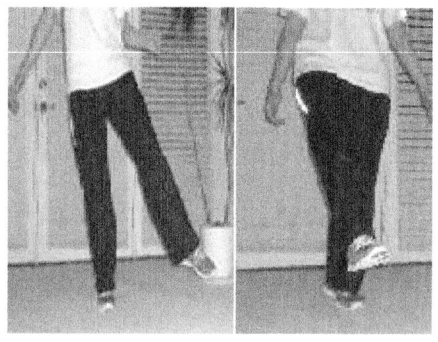

When ankle-ing, you want to go out and around in a circle.

- Karaoke (otherwise known as the grapevine)

    - While standing you want to cross one leg in front of the other and then vice versa, each step moving your body sideways.

When you have the hang of it, start to do it faster- much like you are running.

- Do this for 100 m or 328 ft or time-wise about 40-60 seconds. If you do the drill particularly fast then a lesser time is all right as well.

- Change directions (the leg following before will now become the leg leading) afterwards and repeat the entire thing. An easy way to do this is to simply go in the opposite direction (Point B to Point A if Point A was where you initially started) while facing the same way.

- A more advanced variation would be lifting the knee of the leading leg (the one going over the other) for each crossover. The distance does not change. Make sure to do the drill in the opposite direction as well.

- Toes and Heels
    - Toes.
        - Walk on your toes for 100 m or 328 ft or 2 minutes.
    - Heels.
        - Walk on the heels of your feet for 100 m or 328 ft or for a little over 2 minutes.

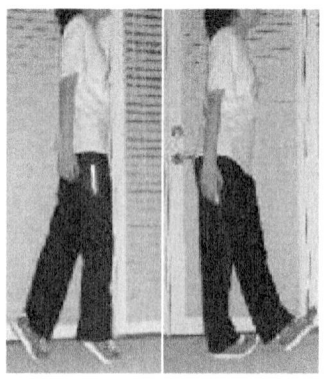

- Toe Touches

- Place one foot in front of the other and keep your toes in the air (keep your heel on the ground). Keep this leg extended straight. Take the hand opposite of the foot with the toes in the air and bend over to touch your toes (on the outstretched leg). Hold for about 5 seconds and switch legs to do the same with the opposite arm. This should make a walking motion.
    - You should feel the stretch here.
    - Do this for about 75 m or 246 ft (or time-wise about 3 minutes because it is a slower exercise).
    - Make sure to do this slowly! This drill involves some stretching-like parts, so remember "bouncing" when stretching is dangerous!
- High Kicks
    - No, we aren't talking about can-can type kicks.
    - Extend both of your arms so they are straight out in front of you. Now kick one foot at a time so that you hit the

hand directly above it. Do the other foot now. This alternating pattern should result in a walking motion, however slow that may be.

- Do this for about 25 m or 82 ft or time-wise about 3 minutes.

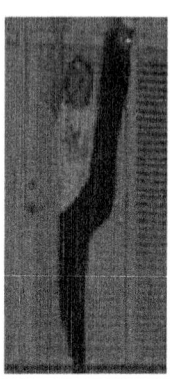

- Hand Walks

  - Prerequisite: You MUST be able to touch your toes to do this drill.

  - Start by bending over and touching your toes (be sure to keep your legs straight). Then keeping your feet where they are, slowly walk (by placing one in front of the other) your hands out until you lower yourself into a pushup position.

From this position, now walk your legs (while keeping your hands in the same place) back up to your hands. Keep your legs straight during this process. Repeat this.

- Do this for about 25 m.

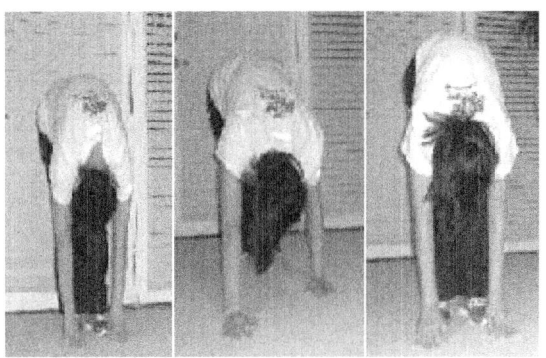

- Strides
  - As mentioned earlier, strides are the length of the distance of your steps you take when you run. And, you want long strides. This is a drill to help with that.
  - For 100 m or 328 ft (or at least a good bit of flat ground) you want to practice these strides. You basically want to run, but you want to focus on reaching out farther with your legs when you are

running. You want sort of a "bounce" in your step when doing this- you literally want to go up vertically a little more than you normally would in running. Take a minute rest after you do one set of strides, and then do two more.
- o Between the second and third set of strides, you only get a 30 second break. (This helps with practicing distance. You don't get a break in the middle of the race, and you want to be striding the entire time.)
- o As time goes on you should decrease the break time little by little.
- Sprinting
  - o This is when you run as fast as you can; it cannot be supported for too long of a time or distance though.
  - o Used mostly in the end of the race; although, some like to sprint in the beginning as well (I don't recommend that.).
  - o To start out this drill, you want to stand on your toes. Then, lean forward as far

as you can. Do not be scared of falling, because it is an automatic response that your foot will come out to catch you when you reach that point. The point where your foot comes out to catch you is the point where you should be leaning when you are sprinting. Any further would not be as aerodynamic in running (and thus reduce speed) and might entail a fall.

- When you're sprinting, you want gravity to be helping you with your speed so you can go faster. Leaning makes your feet go out automatically and very quickly, so you can use most of your energy on kicking off the ground and powering your body towards the finish line.
- Don't do this leaning approach in the beginning of a race (if you are planning on sprinting at the start), because chances are you will lean too soon, and your foot will come out before the gun sounds to initiate the start of the race. If

your foot crosses the start line you will be disqualified. Don't take that chance.

Tilt/lean forward before you start to sprint

- o Now back to the drill. When your foot strikes to catch you from your lean, this is when you should start sprinting. Combine a more moderate version of striding with intense arm pumping, techniques from the A's and B's drills, and basically whatever it takes for you to get to the end as fast as possible. This is the time when you can put all of your drill techniques to trial.

- o Give yourself about a minute of rest, and then do one more set of this sprinting.

- I would also recommend doing the leaning and catching portion of the drill about 5 times. It's important to know where the point that your foot automatically comes out is. If you don't lean far enough in races that won't come to your advantage; you'd just be leaning forward. (Rarely will you lean too much in races, so if there is any doubt, just lean a little more.)

Chapter 5: What to Eat, Drink, and Do Before a Workout, Long Run, or Easy Run

Here are some basic tips on how to eat, drink, and know what to do before a run.

- Eating Tips:
    - You always want to make sure you eat something before you run. You don't want to faint or get dizzy. Not only is that not good in itself, but it also proves for a bad training session. You also need the energy to run.
    - I suggest eating 2-5 hours before running. Always make sure to allow sufficient time for your stomach to digest the food before running. You want to make sure the blood returns from the stomach and back to the muscles in your body.
        - The time frame usually depends on your metabolism. The 2-5-hour timeline is just a guideline. It can deviate a lot from that time

frame; you just have to figure out which is best for you. Just try to find the perfect time to eat before and stick to that- you don't want to eat too early or too late. (For example, thirty minutes before is the best time for me, because I have a fast metabolism.)
- Some food I recommend to eat before a run (light and full of carbohydrates, which supply most of your energy):
  - Sandwiches (basic kind with a very small number of ingredients)
    - Especially with peanut butter and jelly, because peanut butter has protein and fruit jelly has vitamins and antioxidants.
  - Any type of fruit (dried or fresh)
  - Nuts (especially almonds)
  - Granola bars (fruit and nut kind especially)
    - Try to stay away from the more sugary kind and stick

with the more natural and organic type.
- Cereal with milk
  - Opt for whole grain cereal, and milk has calcium which is good for the bones (and as a runner you don't want to hurt your bones).
- Whole grain snacks (like pretzels and crackers)
- Energy Bars (like Power bars, Cliff bars, etc.)
  - I personally do not like the taste of these and reserve them for before and after races and sometimes (rarely) after workouts.
- These are just some of the foods that generally work well for everybody. Remember that every person is different, and a certain food could work best for you and

not at all for someone else. You just have to try for yourself.
- Drinking:
  - Always make sure you drink plenty of fluids- and not just when you're sick!
  - You want to drink a little by little amount of water throughout the day. This will keep you hydrated and will benefit your running.
    - A dehydrated runner will see about a 25% decrease in performance, more or less depending on the person.
    - By the time you are thirsty, you are already well on your way to becoming dehydrated, so make sure to drink plenty even when you are not thirsty.
    - You know you are well hydrated when you have to make a bathroom trip at least once every hour and your urine is clear.
    - Try not to drink TOO much. You know you've reached this point if

you can feel and hear the water moving in your stomach as you move. Different people have different metabolism rates and this point varies.

- Watch out for hyponatremia (also known as water intoxication)! This occurs when you drink too much water and it upsets your salt concentration in your body, making it extremely low. The symptoms are a lot like dehydration because you get nausea, muscle weakness, and dizziness.
  - To prevent this, make sure you eat and drink enough salt throughout the day. (I recommend occasionally drinking juice or sports drinks throughout the day. Consistently drinking them gives you an excess amount of that and

calories, which lead to fat which slow down runners.)
- I recommend about an hour to an hour and a half before you run that you drink about 2 cups (or 16 oz) of water or sports drink to hydrate correctly for the run.
  - Actually, any type of liquid that is not a soft drink should be okay. *Soft drinks, soda, etc. do the opposite of hydrating. They dehydrate your body. Stay away from them when it comes time to run.
- Weigh yourself before you go out to run!
  - When you run, you will lose a percentage of your body weight in sweat. This works towards dehydration, because your body is losing water, and it's mostly made of water.
  - So, you should weigh yourself before and after you run. Weighing before allows you to know the original weight you

were and afterwards tells you how much water you need to drink to get back to your original weight.
- What to Do Before You Run Checklist
    - Eat
    - Drink
    - Stretch
    - Warm-up
    - Drills
    - Dress appropriately for the weather
        - If in doubt, less is better as your body will warm up when you run.
    - Double knot your shoes! You don't want them to come untied in the middle- you will have to stop to tie them and that would mess up the run (unless it's an easy run).

Chapter 6: Running Schedules (Beginners, Intermediate, and Advanced)

Now that you have all the necessary preparations done, it is time to actually run.

The workouts and schedules I am about to give you are assuming that you have a marked (distance-wise) 400-meter track and a 250 m- 300 m hill with a semi-steep grade with a flat surface at the top of the hill that extends for about 100 m. (It is essential to have the flat surface at the top of the hill, while the exact grade and distance of the hill are not as important.)

The workout intensities will be separated into three groups: beginner, intermediate, and advanced.

If the pace is not written, then assume it is to be run at a medium pace (fast enough that you cannot carry an on-going conversation but slow enough you can say comprehensible sentences and you are not out of breath).

Each group will get a 6-week rotation schedule for training. They all contain basically the same type of workouts but at different levels. After 3-4 weeks you may advance to the next group if you feel the schedule is becoming too easy.

In NO case will you advance to the next level after less than 2 weeks. You have a very high chance of injury if you do.

If you want to increase the difficulty of your workout after 4-6 weeks of advanced training, then add a mile onto each distance/long run every 2 weeks up to 15 miles. Leave the easy runs the same distance. For workouts you may increase the distance, but do not go over 10-11 hill repeats or 6-7 one-mile repeats. After that you will start to just increase the pace and lower your times for the workouts.

If you are unable to run the entire distance given to you on the schedule, you may walk or lower the distance by ½ - 1 mile.

The beginners schedule is assuming you are capable of running 2-3 miles continuously already.

If you cannot, then I recommend running ½ - 1 mile three times a week and then increasing it by ½ - 1 mile every week until you can. Then, you should start the beginners' schedule.

I would recommend only running the beginner's schedule once, because the hill workouts are not included in that schedule (the other workouts are more essential than hill workouts). However, to run a 5k well, you must do hill workouts.

You may also keep repeating the 6-week schedule if desired. However, I recommend that you move up a level after repeating the schedule twice.

All distances except those done on the track will be given to you in miles. If you would like to estimate the distances with km, then 1 mile = 1.852 km. In addition, four laps on a 400 m track equal approximately one mile.

After the schedules, I will go into detail about the workouts, long runs, and easy runs.

Beginner's Schedule:

- **Week 1 (16 miles total)**
    - Sunday: Run 3 miles total (including the one mile warm up and one mile cool down so the run is basically 2 miles)
    - Monday: Run 4 miles total (including the warm up and cool down (1- 1½ miles each))
    - Tuesday: Rest Day (do not do any running or gym training)
    - Wednesday: Run 4 miles total (including the warm up and cool down (1- 1 ½ miles))
    - Thursday: Rest Day
    - Friday: Run 5 miles total (including the warm up and cool down)
    - Saturday: Rest Day
- **Week 2: (19 miles total)**
    - Sunday: Run 4 miles total (including warm up and cool down)

- Monday: Run 3 miles total (including warm up and cool down)
- Tuesday: Easy day. Pick an activity or two from the "Change it up" section of the eBook, and do it for a total of 15 minutes.
- Wednesday: Run 3 miles total (including the warm up and the cool down).
- Thursday: Run 5 miles total (including the warm up and the cool down).
- Friday: Rest day
- Saturday: Run 4 miles total (including the warm up and cool down)

- **Week 3: (22 miles total)**
  - Sunday: Run 4 miles total (including warm up and cool down)
  - Monday: Run 5 miles total (including the warm up and cool down)
  - Tuesday: Easy day. Do 15 minutes total of activities mentioned in the "change it up" section.
  - Wednesday: Run 3 miles total (including the warm up and cool down)
  - Thursday: Run 6 miles total (including the warm up and cool down)

- Friday: Rest Day
- Saturday: Run 4 miles total (including the warm up and cool down)

- **Week 4: (26 miles total)**
  - Sunday: Run 5 miles total (including the warm up and cool down)
  - Monday: Run 4 miles total (including the warm up and cool down)
  - Tuesday: Easy day. Do 20 minutes of cross training (the activities listed under the "change it up" section)
  - Wednesday: Run 6 miles total (including the warm up and cool down)
  - Thursday: Run 4 miles total (including the warm up and cool down)
  - Friday: Rest Day (no running or cross training)
  - Saturday: Run 7 miles total (including the warm up and cool down)

- **Week 5: (31 miles total)**
  - Sunday: (On a 400 m track) Run a one mile warm up, and then run 4 miles at a medium pace (faster than jogging but still easy enough where you can hold a simple two-

word exchange with someone else the entire time). Do 6 100m strides with 15 second rest breaks in between. Run a one mile cool down.
- Monday: Run 6 miles total (including warm up and cool down)
- Tuesday: Easy day. 15 minutes of cross training ("change it up" section)
- Wednesday: Run 5 miles total at an easy-medium pace (including warm up and cool down)
- Thursday: Run 6 miles total (including warm up and cool down)
- Friday: Rest day (no running or cross training).
- Saturday: Run 8 miles total (including warm up and cool down) for an endurance run.

- **Week 6: (31 miles total)**
  - Sunday: Run 7 miles at an easy pace (mostly a jogging pace) including the warm up and cool down.
  - Monday: Run a one mile warm up. Run 7 sets of a 40 second speed workout, with 2

½ minutes of recovery (jogging or resting) in between each. Run 1 mile for the cool down.
- Tuesday: Easy day. 25 minutes of cross training (from the "change it up" section)
- Wednesday: Run a one mile warm up. Run three sets of one-mile repeats, and you get a 2-minute recovery (jogging or resting) in between each. Run a 1 mile cool down.
- Thursday: Run 6 miles total (including cool down and warm up) at an easy pace (jogging).
- Friday: Rest day (no running).
- Saturday: Run 8 miles total (including cool down and warm up) for an endurance run.

Intermediate Schedule:

- **Week One: (34 miles total)**
  - Sunday: Run 4 miles total (including warm up and cool down, which should be 1- 1 ½ miles each) for an easy run (basically a little faster than jogging)

- Monday: Run 7 miles total (including the warm up and cool down (1- 1 ½ miles) at a medium pace.
- Tuesday: Rest Day
- Wednesday: Run 7 miles total (including the warm up and cool down (1 -1 ½ miles)).
- Thursday: Run 5 miles total (including warm up and cool down) at an easy pace (about jogging pace)
- Friday: Run 8 miles total (including warm up and cool down).
- Saturday: Run 3 miles total (including warm up and cool down)

- **Week Two (about 32 miles total)**
  - Sunday: Run 6 miles total (including warm up and cool down) at an easy pace (around jogging speed).
  - Monday: (On a 400 m track.) Run a 1 mile warm up. Run 3 miles at an easy run pace. Do strides (as directed in the "Drills" section) for 100 m. Repeat 6 times with a 200 m recovery (slow jog) in between each repetition. Run a 1 mile cool down.

- o Tuesday: Run 6 miles total (including warm up and cool down) at an easy run pace.
- o Wednesday: Run a 1 mile warm up. Sprint for 40 seconds and rest for 2 minutes and 30 seconds (slow jog). Repeat this 8 times. Run a 1 mile cool down.
- o Thursday: Rest Day!
- o Friday: Run 8 miles total (including warm up and cool down) for an endurance run.
- o Saturday: Easy day! Do cross training (pick an activity or two from the "change it up" section) for 20 minutes.

- **Week Three: (about 41 miles total)**
  - o Sunday: Run 6 miles total (including warm up and cool down) at an easy pace (jogging).
  - o Monday: Run a 1 mile warm up. Sprint for 40 seconds and take 2 minutes and 30 seconds for recovery (slow jog). Repeat this 8 times. Run a 1 mile cool down.
  - o Tuesday: Run 7 miles total (including warm up and cool down) at an easy pace (jogging).

- Wednesday: Run a 1 mile warm up. Run three one-mile repeats with 2-minute recoveries in between each (slow jogging recoveries). Run a 1 mile cool down.
- Thursday: Run 6 miles total (including warm up and cool down) at an easy run pace (jogging).
- Friday: Run 8 miles total (including warm up and cool down) as an endurance run.
- Saturday: Run 5 miles total (including warm up and cool down) at an easy run pace.

- **Week Four: (about 43 miles total)**
  - Sunday: Run a 1 mile warm up. Sprint for 40 seconds and rest for 2 minutes and 30 seconds recovery (slow jog). Repeat this TEN times. Run a 1 mile cool down.
  - Monday: Run 6 miles total (including warm up and cool down) at an easy run pace (jogging pace).
  - Tuesday: Run 8 miles total (including warm up and cool down) for an endurance run.

- Wednesday: Run 5 miles total (including warm up and cool down) at an easy run pace (jogging pace).
- Thursday: (On a 400 m track.) Run a 1 mile warm up. Run 3 miles at an easy run pace (jogging). Do strides (as indicated in the "drills" section) for 100 meters. Give yourself a 200-meter recovery period (jogging). Run a 1 mile cool down.
- Friday: Run 9 miles total (including warm up and cool down) as an endurance run.
- Saturday: Run 5 miles total (including warm up and cool down) at an easy run pace (jogging).

- **Week Five: (about 41 miles total)**
  - Sunday: Run 7 miles total (including warm up and cool down) at an easy run pace (jogging pace).
  - Monday: Run a 1 mile warm up. Sprint for 40 seconds and give yourself 2 minutes and 20 seconds for recovery (slow jogging). Repeat this ten times. Run a 1 mile cool down.

- Tuesday: Run 6 miles total (including warm up and cool down) at an easy run pace (jogging).
- Wednesday: Run a 1 mile warm up. Run three one-mile repeats with 1 minute and 30 seconds recovery time (slow jogging) in between each repeat. Run a 1 mile cool down.
- Thursday: Run 7 miles total (including warm up and cool down) at an easy run pace (jogging).
- Friday: Run 10 miles total (including warm up and cool down) as an endurance run.
- Saturday: Rest Day!

- **Week Six: (about 38 miles total)**
  - Sunday: Run 6 miles total (including warm up and cool down) at an easy run pace (jogging).
  - Monday: (On a 250 m- 300 m hill with a flat portion at the top that goes for 100 m.) Run a 1 mile warm up on a flat area. Run up the hill 3 times continuously- no break or recovery time. Each time you get to the top of the hill start doing strides (as indicated in

the "Drills" section) for the 100 m on top. Run a 1 mile cool down of a flat area.
- Tuesday: Run 5 miles total (including the warm up and cool down) at an easy run pace (jogging).
- Wednesday: Run a one mile warm up. Run three one-mile repeats with a one minute and 30 second recoveries (slow jogging). Run a 1 mile cool down.
- Thursday: Run 7 miles total (including the warm up and cool down) at an easy run pace (jogging).
- Friday: Run 11 miles total (including the warm up and cool down) as an endurance run.

Advanced Schedule:

- **Week One: (45 total miles)**
  - Sunday: Run 6 miles total (including warm up and cool down (which should each be 1 mile to 1 ½ miles)) at an easy run pace (a little faster than a jogging pace).

- Monday: Run a 1 mile warm up. Sprint (run as fast as you can) for 40 seconds. Recover with a 2 minute and 30 second slow jog. Repeat this TEN times. Run a 1 mile cool down.
- Tuesday: Run 8 miles total (including warm up and cool down (1 -1 ½ mi)) at an easy run pace (jogging).
- Wednesday: Run a 1 mile warm up. Run a mile with a 2-minute recovery (slow jog). Repeat this three times. Run a 1 mile cool down.
- Thursday: Run 6 miles total (including warm up and cool down) at an easy run pace (jogging).
- Friday: Run 8 miles total (including warm up and cool down) for an endurance run.
- Saturday: Run 7 miles total (including warm up and cool down) at an easy run pace (jogging).

- **Week Two: (about 38 total miles)**
  - Sunday: (On a 400 m track or just estimated striding distances.) Run 8 miles

- total (including warm up and cool down) at an easy run pace (jogging).
  - Monday: Run a 1 mile warm up. Run 4 miles at an easy run pace (jogging). Do 7 sets of strides (as instructed in the "Drills" section) for 100 m with a 200 m recovery in between each (slow jogging). Run a 1 mile cool down.
  - Tuesday: Run 8 miles total (including warm up and cool down) at an easy run pace (jogging).
  - Wednesday: Run a 1 mile warm up. Sprint for 40 seconds and recover for 2 minutes and 30 seconds with a slow jog. Repeat this NINE times. Run a 1 mile cool down.
  - Thursday: Easy day: Spend 20 minutes doing cross training (pick an activity or two from the "Change it Up" section). Make sure to stretch.
  - Friday: Run 9 miles total (including warm up and cool down) as an endurance run.
  - Saturday: REST DAY! (THAT MEANS NO RUNNING- not even if you want!!)
- **Week Three: (about 48 total miles)**

- Sunday: Run 6 miles total (including warm up and cool down) at an easy run pace (jogging).
- Monday: Run a 1 mile warm up. Sprint for 40 seconds and then take a 2 minute and 30 second recovery (slow jogging). Repeat this ELEVEN times. Run a 1 mile cool down.
- Tuesday: Run 7 miles total (including warm up and cool down) at an easy run pace (jogging).
- Wednesday: Run 8 miles total (including warm up and cool down) as an endurance run.
- Thursday: (On a 400 m track or estimated distance.) Run a 1 mile warm up. Run 4 miles at an easy run pace (jogging). Do 7 sets of 100 m strides (as instructed in the "Drills" section) with 200 m recoveries in between (slow jogging). Run a 1 mile cool down.
- Friday: Run 9 miles total (including warm up and cool down) as an endurance run.

- Saturday: Run 7 miles total (including warm up and cool down) at an easy run pace (jogging).
- **Week Four: (about 50 miles total)**
  - Sunday: Run 8 miles total (including warm up and cool down) at an easy run pace (jogging).
  - Monday: Run a 1 mile warm up. Sprint for 40 seconds and take a 2 minute and 15 second recovery (slow jog). Repeat this TEN times. Run a 1 mile cool down.
  - Tuesday: Run 6 miles total (including warm up and cool down) at an easy run pace (jogging).
  - Wednesday: Run a 1 mile warm up. Run 1 mile and take a 1 minute and 20 second recovery (slow jogging). Repeat this three times. Run a 1 mile cool down.
  - Thursday: Run 8 miles total (including warm up and cool down) at an easy run pace (jogging).
  - Friday: Run 10 miles total (including warm up and cool down) as an endurance run.

- Saturday: Run 6 miles total (including warm up and cool down) at an easy run pace (jogging).
- **Week Five: (about 49 miles total)**
  - Sunday: Run 6 miles total (including warm up and cool down) at an easy run pace (jogging).
  - Monday: (On a 250 – 300 m hill with a 100 m flat area at the top.) Run 1 mile warm up. Run up the hill 3 times (your recovery is on the way down so you can slow jog that portion). When you get to the top (without a break) stride the 100 m flat area (as instructed in the "Drills" section). Recover on the way back. Run a 1 mile cool down.
  - Tuesday: Run a 1 mile warm up. Sprint 40 seconds and recover 2 minutes and 10 seconds (slow jog). Repeat this TWELVE times. Run a 1 mile cool down.
  - Wednesday: Run 11 miles total (including warm up and cool down) as an endurance run.

- Thursday: Run 4 miles total (including warm up and cool down) at an easy run pace (jogging).
- Friday: Run 11 miles total (including warm up and cool down) at an easy run pace (jogging).
- Saturday: Run 7 miles total (including warm up and cool down) at an easy run pace (jogging).

- **Week Six: (about 44 miles total)**
  - Sunday: Run 7 miles total (including warm up and cool down) at an easy run pace (jogging).
  - Monday: (On a 250 – 300 m hill with a 100 m flat area at the top.) Run a 1 mile warm up. Run up the hill and stride (according to the instructions in the "Drills" section) the 100 m flat section when you get to the top. After the stride, run that distance twice (once back and then half in and half out) so it's 200 m of recovery (at a slow jog pace) and then run down the hill again. Repeat this FIVE times. Run a 1 mile cool down.

- Tuesday: Run 6 miles total (including warm up and cool down) at an easy run pace (jogging).
- Wednesday: Run a 1 mile warm up. Run 1 mile and take a 1 minute and 30 second recovery (slow jog). Repeat this FOUR times. Run a 1 mile cool down.
- Thursday: Easy Day (15 minutes of cross training (activity from "Change It Up" section) or REST DAY. Your choice.
- Friday: Run 12 miles total (including warm up and cool down) as an endurance run.
- Saturday: Run 8 miles total (including warm up and cool down) at an easy run pace (jogging).

Chapter 7: Training in Detail

Easy Runs:

For easy runs you want to relax. The easy run pace's definition can be simply be put as "a little faster than jogging" speed. Looking more closely into it, you should focus on your leg strides, breathing, and running form.

When you are running an easy run pace, you want to be able to inhale and exhale really deeply. (Remember the "Diaphragmatic Breathing" taught in Chapter Two's Running basics? Think about that while running.) You want to hold your breath intakes in as long as possible and push the air out for as long as possible. This relaxes your entire body and makes your oxygen exchange more efficient.

The point of easy runs is more than just to give you a break from long endurance runs and workouts. Easy runs allow you to practice relaxed running. When you run a lot of easy runs, as all three schedules from the previous chapter have incorporated, your body and mind get used to the idea of relaxed muscles and efficient oxygen exchange. This will soon become habit, and this is a good running habit to have. When you're running a race, you do not want to have to think about this stuff.

Make sure to have good running posture and form! Remember arms are at 90 degrees about and your entire body is standing up "naturally straight"- not too straight but NEVER hunched over. Keep your head straight up and looking straight!!

Remember to make your leg strides long! You want to be able to cover as much distance as you can with every step. This helps with efficient energy use and by doing so you make yourself go faster.

A good pace for running easy runs (besides just judging "jogging paces") is to try to talk while you are running. You should be able to mostly carry on a conversation- but not ongoing. You should not be "huffing" and "puffing" while trying to gasp in air as a result of talking. You shouldn't be able to drone on and on either- you are running!

If you are able to talk endlessly and continuously, then you are going too slowly. It's an easy run, but it is still part of training!

Easy runs are allowed to be interrupted frequently for stretch breaks. If you are getting an easy day most likely you just had a difficult workout or you have one coming up. Take advantage of the easy day to stretch and run to loosen up and relax your muscles.

- Time-wise, I would recommend running:
  - Starters: 20-25 minutes a mile
  - Beginner level (as indicated by the schedule in the previous chapter): 15 – 16 minutes a mile
  - Intermediate level (as indicated by the schedule in the previous chapter): 13- 14 minutes a mile

- Advanced level (as indicated by the schedule in the previous chapter): 10-12 minutes a mile.
- I know everyone is capable of running these times, BUT you have to remember this is an EASY run. This is time to give your muscles a little bit of a break- although you still have to run- and work on your breathing and running form. I recommend staying within those times to stay relaxed and not strain your muscles.

Endurance Runs:

Endurance runs are NOT the same as easy runs. This was not specified in the schedule, but be SURE to remember and know the difference. Exactly as the name implies, these are to build up your endurance. You need endurance to run the 5k!

Endurance runs are supposed to build up your legs and body's tolerance to increased mileage. After doing about 10 miles at one time all of a sudden, the 3.1 miles of a 5k race are no longer that bad anymore. This helps with your mindset and your body. Once you can do longer distances, then you can start to increase the speed on the shorter distances and most importantly the race distance.

Do NOT interrupt any of your endurance runs with multiple (or any for that matter) stretch breaks unless they are absolutely necessary. Stretching can be done throughout the designated warm up and cool down (1 - 1 1/2 miles each) portion of the total endurance run distance.

You want to keep a moderate or endurance pace during this run. Breathing wise you should be able to utter about a sentence or something at a time but not much more past that. You should not be TOO strained but this is no easy run. You may have to catch your breath after talking but by no means is gasping necessary. You are going too fast if you have to gasp at all (or you are talking too much).

Endurance and distance running builds muscle and tones. This is why you don't always do workouts. Runners don't want to become "bulky" they want to be toned so you don't have to carry as much weight when you run and the weight you do carry is mostly muscle so that muscle helps you to run faster.

If you run too slowly for endurance runs (even if the distance is exactly the same) then you just lose fat and use up carbohydrates- the muscle building and toning is not as much.

When doing long runs, you want to pay attention especially to your form. If you do your form correctly, it should make the running somewhat easier and more natural. You never want to feel like you're forcing yourself too much- although you are obviously moving your legs it should not be forced step by step.

This is a good time to put all of your easy runs and drills to work. You want to be able to keep doing the techniques like the [Part] A's and [Part] B's while keeping your form for as long as possible. If you can keep that form and if you do keep that the entire endurance run you will certainly be able to do so during a race.

I understand long runs are difficult, but you always want to make it look like it's easy. Any bystander looking at you run should think what you are doing is not very difficult and they could do the same. The point is that it IS VERY difficult, and they most likely could not. However, this is how your running motions should look.

If you are keeping correct running form and are running "naturally" by not forcing yourself and making smooth and clean footsteps (again think A's and B's in a less exaggerated way), then it should look easy.

You have to be relaxed in order for your run to "look" easy. If you are tense and rigid you can see it in your arms, legs, shoulder, and face. It requires a lot more energy to move your muscles in running if you are tense and are using energy to "fight" your forward motion. Instead of using energy to hold back your body, you should use it to propel you forward so you finish the 5k faster.

This is why great runners (and athletes in general) always make something that is very difficult look very easy and simple. They know the secret- make something look easy and it will truly become easier. If you make it look easy you are doing it right and well. And, if you are doing it right and well, then it will make it a little easier and you will be better.

- Running times for endurance runs:

    o Starters: 17 - 18 minutes a mile.

    o Beginners (as indicated by the schedule in the previous chapter): 14 - 16 minutes a mile.

    o Intermediate (as indicated by the schedule in the previous chapter): 11 - 13 minutes a mile.

    o Advanced (as indicated by the schedule in the previous chapter): 7 – 10 minutes a mile.

    o I really would not recommend running 7 minutes a mile for endurance runs- even if you are perfectly capable of running 15 miles at that pace. It's an endurance run not a workout. You are building up endurance, so you should use about 70 -

75% effort here. No need to use more than that.

Workouts

There are four workouts I included in the schedules from the previous chapter. These are the four that I find the most effective and time worthy (especially if you're strapped for time).

The Mile Repeat

This is where you run a mile (about 1600 m) as a workout and you do this multiple times.

This is my absolute favorite workout. I think this is the most beneficial (if the 5k race you are running is mostly flat, which most are). The least amount of repeats you should ever run with these should be 3. The most should be around 6 – 7. I normally like to do around 5, and after a while you just increase the speed as you get better and better.

The recovery time I usually take is around 1 minute and 15 seconds if I am feeling up to it that day. We all have our not-so-good running days and on those I usually allow myself 1 minute and 30 seconds of recovery. Unless you are a beginner or starter you should ALWAYS be taking slow jog recoveries NOT stand still ones.

This is for the same reason they tell you to keep walking after a long run, workout, race, etc. You want to keep moving so you don't get lactic acid (the stuff that cause burning in your legs during and after intense running) stuck in your legs, and you want to keep moving because you were just running intensely and an immediate stop is never going to be good for you.

And, doing a slow jog instead of just stopping requires more endurance. Slow jogging allows you to recover, but you never really stop running.

This teaches you to slow jog if you feel like you HAVE to stop. If you're running a race and you feel terrible all of a sudden, you will remember that a slow jog during workouts is enough of a recovery to go on. It's MUCH better to slow jog than to completely stop in a race.

And, when you completely stop to recover this means you have to start all over again. This plays with your mindset and proves to be much more difficult than just increasing your speed from a slow jog.

Remember your mind can make you go farther and faster than your body ever could!

During mile repeats, you want to be on a 400 m track or in a place where you can figure out how far a mile is. (On a 400 m track it is 4 complete laps.)

You want to have long strides (Remember the techniques taught in the "Drills" section!) and you want to be aggressively pumping your arms. This will help you go faster and make sure you have good running form!!

Remember to breathe in your nose and out your mouth and elongate it as much as possible!

- Recommended times for Mile Repeats:
  - Starters: 13:00 – 15:59 minutes a mile.
  - Beginners (as indicated by the schedule in the previous chapter): 10:00 – 12:59 minutes a mile.
  - Intermediate (as indicated by the schedule in the previous chapter): 7:00-9:59 minutes a mile.
  - Advanced (as indicated by the schedule in the previous chapter): 5:00 – 6:59 minutes a mile.
  - If you can do 6 to 7 repeats of a 5:00 minute mile, then I would still recommend you do not go much faster than that unless that time is EXTREMEMLY easy for you. There's no need to put too much strain in this workout. It is a workout, but you don't need to give 100 % effort.

- - I don't mean you don't need to try as hard as you can, but you don't need to completely wear yourself out to the point of exhaustion. I think about 80 – 85% is sufficient for this workout.
  - These times are just approximate time frames to be used as guidelines. They do not have to be followed exactly. Each person is different.

The Forty Second Sprints

This is where you sprint (run as fast as you can) for forty seconds. The distances vary from person to person and depend on how fast you run. Therefore, the easiest way to increase your difficulty is to run faster or sprint faster. Of course, you are sprinting so you should be going as fast as you possibly can for that distance.

You should not be going as fast as a bullet the first 10 seconds and then slow jogging the last 30 seconds, because you completely wore yourself out. You need to slow down enough that you can "push" or "will yourself" to finish the entire forty seconds at that pace.

If you cannot keep a pace for forty seconds, then you need to slow it down. When you sprint in a 5k race, you will need to sprint for forty seconds or longer in the beginning or end. (In the beginning it gets you in front of the walkers and slower runners and at the end it helps you beat other runners at the last minute and get a better time.) You want to be able to hold a very fast pace for as long as you can.

I typically take a two-minute recovery in between (slow jogging)- if you want something to judge it by other than the schedule.

I recommend practicing the "Sprinting Drill" as indicated in the "Drills" section, especially the leaning start.

You want to make sure you are pumping your arms especially fast and hard, because you are sprinting here. When you sprint, you want shorter steps than the normal distance running steps. The [Part] A as indicated in the "Drills" section is what you should be mimicking here (as opposed to the [Part] B's you normally use when running the majority of the 5k).

I would not go over 15 repeats of this workout (the schedules only go up to 12 on the advanced). Beyond there you should just start running faster for the forty seconds. The intended race being prepared for is the 5k, and you do not need to do more than 15 repeats for 5k training.

I typically do around 11 repeats of this exercise, because I personally would rather increase the speed than the repetitions. This depends on the person, so find out what works better for you. Whatever seems "easier" to your mind is what you should stick to. You want to keep your "Runner's Mindset" advantage.

You don't want to do much less than 8 of these repetitions, because this workout is especially useful in the middle of races when you need to pass people.

When you're in the middle of the race and you see someone in front of your struggling, breathing heavily, dropping their arms, losing their running form, or any other number or indicators of slowing down, you will need to surge for about forty seconds to pass them and get enough in front of them that if they get motivated and start to pick up the pace you are far enough ahead that they cannot catch you.

Another reason to keep your running form and posture and not to tense up is that some other runners will be able to see these "tell-tale" signs and they will surge to pass you. Even if you are struggling you have to make it look easy and make it look like you're doing just fine.

The Easy Run And Strides

This is not really considered a workout, but I think the strides part after the easy run is VERY important.

Strides are essential to doing well in races. Good runners always have long strides, because they want to cover more distance in one step so they can go faster with less energy used.

Practicing strides usually also helps with running form as well.

The easy run before the strides should make you a little tired from running, but you should have enough energy to do strides correctly. Those exaggerated strides (in the drills and here) are not too tiring, and your body will remember this when you are running.

You should have less exaggerated strides, which is exactly what you need, during races. There is no recommending timing for this.

The Hill Repeats With Strides

When running hills in races, most people will slow down. This is exactly why you must SPEED UP when you see a hill. You are able to pass so many people on hills.

A lot of people know they have to run up the hill at a decent speed or they will get passed, but most people slow down when they reach the top of the hill. Their bodies automatically feel that they need to recover, and this is when you should take the chance to pass them.

You need to run these workouts up a 250 – 300 m hill, because these are usually the medium to large size hills in 5k races. (Of course, there are always exceptions though.) You want to go up the hills as fast as you can, going the fastest and focusing the most on the middle section and the top portion- people tend to go fast in the beginning.

When you get to the top of the hill and reach the 100 m flat area, you want to pick up the pace immediately. I know you will feel like you're especially tired from the hill, but trust me on this one. It's a secret that has enabled me to be successful in 5k races. Start striding (as indicated by the workout and drill) when you hit the top of the hill. Striding picks up the speed and you do not use nearly as much energy as sprinting.

After 100 m of striding, you should run back for a full 100m at a recovery pace (slow jogging) and then turn around to run halfway and then go back again towards the hill, so you have 200m total of recovery time. Then you can also recover while you run down the hill (in work outs ONLY!! You want to use gravity and let yourself go loose in races- don't hold back!).

In races when you reach the top of the hill, you will know that the beginning of the stride will be especially hard but after that 100m your body will calm down and return to normal. The elevated heart rate from the hill will calm down, but you first have to keep it elevated for just 100 m more. Trust me this works every time. Whether you are a faster runner or a slower runner, this is not something that people usually do. You will have the advantage.

Remember running up a hill you want to put your leg at about a 90-degree angle as you climb the hill. Using the [Part] B's from the drills will not help you when you are going up an incline. You want a 90-degree angle to get as much distance covered as possible. You want to pump your arms more into the air when running up hills as well. Lean into the hill a little bit as you are running up and down it.

Rest Days and Cross training

Make sure you take these days easy! You want to make these your days to recover. ICE ICE ICE! If your muscles hurt or even feel a little sore you need to ICE and STRETCH! You don't want an injury- especially after you've worked this hard.

If the schedule says to take an OFF day or REST day, then do NOT run. It's all about preventing injuries and giving your muscles much needed rest. I know you are capable of running on those days, but the rest days are there to help prevent injuries. TAKE THEM!

ALWAYS REMEMBER TO RELAX YOUR BODY AND ELONGATE YOUR BREATHING!

Chapter 8: Race Day!

What to Bring to the Race

Clothing

- In warm weather…
    - Bring 3 pairs of shorts and 3 t-shirts/tank tops or whatever you'd be comfortable with racing in, because you never know if it will rain during and/or before the race. You want to be able to remain dry or at least as dry as possible.
    - Most races start in the morning or you must arrive in the morning, so I recommend wearing a sweatshirt and sweatpants over your racing gear to warm-up in and wear around. Mornings can be cold even in the summer.
- In cool weather…
    - If you would like to race "bundled-up"
        - Bring 2 pairs of long exercise pants and 3 pairs of long-sleeve shirts (racing with these will leave you especially sweaty at the end

so you will want to be able to stay dry afterwards).
- I recommend wearing spandex pants and shirts to race. Underarmour, Nike's dryfit, and other brands or offbrands work nicely. (The majority percentage of the material should be spandex, but a little bit of cotton makes for more comfort.)
- If desired, you may bring a hooded/non-hooded sweatshirt to race in or where before/after the race. If racing with the sweatshirt, bring two.
- If you would like to race without the extra baggage of long-sleeves and pants
  - Wear your racing t-shirt/tank top and shorts underneath hooded/non-hooded sweatshirt and sweatpants to the meet. You may also want to wear a ski jacket or some other sort of large jacket over that combination. You want

to keep warm during your warm-up and stretches.
- Bring two t-shirts/tank tops and shorts to the meet. You always want to bring one extra.
    - If you're unsure which way you would like to race, I recommend bringing two t-shirts/tank tops, a long-sleeve shirt, a pair of long pants for racing, and a pair of shorts.
- Golden Rule of Dress
    - I always make sure to bring a hooded sweatshirt, two or three comfortable t-shirts, two pairs of shorts, one long-sleeve shirt, and a pair of sweatpants (without the elastic on the bottom).
        - I like racing in tank tops or t-shirts (depending on the weather) and shorts. If it's particularly cold I'll consider a long-sleeve, but the extra clothing would be a little heavier and will slow you down somewhat. Choose clothing wisely.

- Sweatpants without elastic on the bottom allow you to take the sweatpants off at the start-line, and they go easily over your shoes. Elastic makes that process more difficult.
- This is what I pack every race, so I 100% recommend this combination.

Accessories

- A watch - most essential accessory! You want to be able to check the time and pace yourself. It helps to "push you" to do your best in the race as well.
- Sunglasses-important if it's especially sunny outside. You may not notice it, but when you're running and the sun shines into your eyes, you automatically slow down a bit.
- Hat- protects your head from excess heat. You may think it will make the situation worse, but

in reality, it protects your head from the sun's heat. You don't want to get overheated.
- For long hair...
    - Bring two elastic hair bands that do not have a metal part. A lot of races will disqualify you if an official sees the metal.
    - Bring an elastic headband without a metal connection part- this too can usually get you disqualified.
    - Bring pre-wrap (the foam-like wrap that goes under athletic tape). Many races allow for you to use this in place of a headband.
        - For correct head sizing, typically you would wrap it once around the upper part of your thigh and tear off that portion. Then, you just tie the ends. Pre-wrap stretches, so it should fit nicely around your head.

Food!

Most races are in the morning, but regardless make sure you eat a good meal before you arrive at the meet. Anything with a lot of carbohydrates and little salt, sugar, and preservatives should be good.

Every person is different in what they can and can't eat before a race. The only way to test this out is to try. If it's your first race, then I'd recommend going for something with whole grains and some fruit and water or juice. Eat this about 2 – ½ hours before.

- What snacks to bring to the meet?
    - Fresh fruit!
    - Bagels, bread, and other things with whole wheat
    - Dried fruit (I would recommend fresh, but some people prefer dried.)
    - Energy or protein bars (I usually bring a PowerBar, but Cliff Bars, and any brand or generic brand should work as long as it has a lot of carbohydrates and protein.)
        - Don't bring a flavor or type that you find unappealing, the last thing you need for your body and mindset is to vomit right before

you start your race or during the race.
- Eat this about 1 hour before you actually run. I typically eat 20 – 30 minutes before I run (or sometimes even sooner), but the vast majority of people have to eat 1 hour before.
  - You want the blood to have time to return from digesting your food in your stomach to their places in your muscles before you race.
  - Eating earlier before a race is always better than eating later.

Pre-Race Tips

You want to get to the meet location about 2 -3 hours before the race starts.

You want to be able to get there and do a warm up, which I usually do by running a mile of the course and walking the rest.

You want to get a feel for the course to know where to go and what to expect, because sometimes the course is not marked well or the spray paint or markers are knocked down or rubbed away by runners as they go through the race.

And, the course is 3.1 miles, so you don't want to run that entire distance before a race. You want to save as much energy as possible. I recommend just running 1 mile (and at most 1 ½ but only if you're used to running that for the warm ups in easy runs and endurance runs).

Now you want to stretch. Do ALL of the stretches in the stretches section.

Now you should go to the bathroom (about 20 – 30 minutes before your race will start). Don't drink anymore water after this period. (You should have been drinking especially the night before and before this time.)

Relax and listen to music or chat with a friend until it's about 15 minutes before your race should start. Walk down to the start line with you racing shoes (spikes or flats) in hand and a bottle of sports drink or water. You should still be wearing your sweatshirt and sweatpants if you chose to.

Do your drills somewhere near the start line. The race may start earlier than the "official start time", and you want to be nearby just in case.

If you are still nervous, then you should do about 5 sit-ups and one pushup to get your adrenaline going and calm your nerves. This also helps with your mindset as it leaves you feeling strong. You don't want to do too many or you'll waste energy.

Now change your shoes to your racing shoes (if you have them) and leave your training shoes and sweatshirt and sweatpants by the start line or with someone you know. (Usually your stuff won't be stolen if you leave it at the start line- unless it's a particularly big meet.)

People should now be walking towards the start line. Find your place and get on the line and wait for the official's instructions. Jump around (up down) a little bit to keep your leg muscles warm and loose.

Time to get into your running stance. This is very much like stretching your calves but without a wall.

Make sure you don't cross over the line before the gun sounds, or you will be "false starting" and could be disqualified.

When The Gun Goes Off...

Now you need to go without thinking. You cannot hesitate right now. You need to get out there as fast as possible! You don't want to get stuck behind, because it's difficult to keep your pace if you're stuck behind a bunch of runners that slow down and cause a blockade.

Be careful and watch out for peoples' spikes and try not to get elbowed or kicked!

Be careful! The beginning of races- especially large ones- has a lot of shoving and people fall. Don't be one of the people that fall.

You want to have a good start but don't go out at a full sprint- this drains energy and you will be very tired the rest of the race.

Remember! You can only LOSE a 5k race in the first mile; you can never WIN a 5k race in the first mile.

Once the runners begin to spread out into their respective groups: leaders, middle, and back, you need to focus on relaxing and elongating your breathing. In your nose and out your mouth as slow as you can.

Remember the Forty Second Sprints? In the middle of the race you will see people slow down or show signs that they are tiring out. Now is the time to surge and practice the workout you've been doing!

For hills, remember to lean into them when going down and up. You want to pump your arms especially up hills and keep a 90-degree knee angle when going up. DON'T LET YOUR HEEL HIT when you are going DOWNHILL! Let yourself go down without hesitating and keep your arms at your side instead of letting them flail.

Remember to stride for about 100 m when you get to the top of the hill!!!!

Remember to keep your speed in the middle of the hill, while most people slow down!

For creeks and other water places, you want to do high knees like in your drills. Relax and run through like that.

Finishing??

Make sure to lean forward like you practiced in the sprinting drill. You want to pump your arms really hard and sprint for 40 seconds like in the workout. You want to give it your all. You will have all the time in the world to rest after you hit that finish line.

Keep your breathing elongated especially here! You don't want your muscles to suddenly run out of oxygen when you're supposed to be finished strong and hard!

Chapter 9: After the Race

After you cross the finish line all you want to do is sit down or lay down. DO NOT!!! You have to keep moving, so just slowly walk around and drink some water or sports drink.

When you feel like you are able to jog again, you need to slowly jog 1 mile for a cool down. You always have to do a cool down- you don't want your muscles hurt!

After your cool down, you need to stretch. NEVER forget to stretch! Stretching helps to prevent injuries.

Now drink a lot of liquid (water or sports drink) and eat some of the food like the protein bars. You especially need protein in your body now.

When you return home, make sure you "eat the rainbow". You want to eat foods that are red, orange, yellow, green, blue, and purple to make sure you replenish your body with all the vitamins and antioxidants and minerals it needs. The race you just ran was very hard on your body, and you want to reward your body for a good job.

I would not recommend running even an easy run or doing cross training the same day after you run a 5k race. Your body just went through a bunch of strain and needs to rest. The next day I would only run a 4-mile total (including warm up and cool down) easy run.

Make sure you stretch A LOT after you run the race and not just immediately afterwards. You need to stretch throughout the day and the next and perhaps the next too.

You don't want to immediately just stop running- even if you only planned on running one 5k. When you do that you will lose a lot of the muscle you just gained from training.

Ideally you would keep running the equivalence of easy runs every day to keep healthy and in shape.

If you plan to stop running altogether after the race, then I recommend you slowly wean yourself off of running by cutting down the mileage every week little by little and only running easy runs. You should take about 1 rest day at first and then make your way to 2, then 3, and finally 7. I don't recommend this, because you will still lose a lot of muscle- but not as much as you would have if you just immediately stopped running.

So, these are the basic tips after the race.

Now, you have learned the basics on how to run and succeed in the 5K race. All you have to do now is to go out there and do it. Apply this knowledge into action. Thanks for reading this guide and I wish you the best of success!

Recommended Resources

- HowExpert.com – Quick 'How To' Guides on All Topics from A to Z by Everyday Experts.
- HowExpert.com/free – Free HowExpert Email Newsletter.
- HowExpert.com/books – HowExpert Books
- HowExpert.com/courses – HowExpert Courses
- HowExpert.com/clothing – HowExpert Clothing
- HowExpert.com/membership – HowExpert Membership Site
- HowExpert.com/affiliates – HowExpert Affiliate Program
- HowExpert.com/writers – Write About Your #1 Passion/Knowledge/Expertise & Become a HowExpert Author.
- HowExpert.com/resources – Additional HowExpert Recommended Resources
- YouTube.com/HowExpert – Subscribe to HowExpert YouTube.
- Instagram.com/HowExpert – Follow HowExpert on Instagram.
- Facebook.com/HowExpert – Follow HowExpert on Facebook.

Printed in Great Britain
by Amazon